# Fabulous Paper Gliders

## Norman Schmidt

Sterling Publishing Co., Inc.  New York
A Sterling/Tamos Book

**A Sterling/Tamos Book**

Sterling Publishing Company, Inc.
387 Park Avenue South, New York, N.Y. 10016

Tamos Books Inc.
300 Wales Avenue, Winnipeg, MB, Canada R2M 2S9

10  9  8  7  6  5  4  3  2  1

© 1998 by Norman Schmidt

*Design:* Norman Schmidt
*Photography:* Jerry Grajewski, Custom Images

Distributed in Canada by Sterling Publishing
% Canadian Manda Group, One Atlantic Avenue, Suite 105
Toronto, Ontario, Canada M6K 3E7
Distributed in Great Britain and Europe by Cassell PLC
Wellington House, 125 Strand, London WC2R 0BB, England
Distributed in Australia by Capricorn Link (Australia) Pty Ltd.
P.O. Box 6651, Baulkham Hills, Business Centre, NSW 2153, Australia


**Canadian Cataloging in Publication Data**
Schmidt, Norman, 1947-

Fabulous Paper Gliders/Norman Schmidt.-

"A Sterling/Tamos book."
Includes index.
ISBN 1-895569-21-4 (bound); 1-895569-23-0 (pbk.)
1. Paper airplanes. I. Title.

TL778.S353 1997    745.592    C97-920115-2


**Library of Congress Cataloging- in-Publication Data Available**


*Printed in China*
*All rights reserved*


Sterling  ISBN    1-895569-21-4  Trade
                  1-895569-23-0  Paper

The advice and directions given in this book have been carefully checked, prior to printing, by the Author as well as the Publisher. Nevertheless, no guarantee can be given as to project outcome due to possible differences in materials and construction and the Author and Publisher will not be responsible for the results.

# Contents

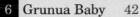

Below: A typical scene at a gliderport. Shown on the flightline are various types of gliders preparing for launch.

Inset: Gliders are not large, most are single seat aircraft having a slender and streamlined profile. Shown is the author with his Schweizer SGS 1-26B.

**M**ANY people are familiar with the story of general aviation, beginning with the historic flight of the Wright brothers in 1903. Motorless flight, however, is less well known, in spite of the fact that motorless planes played a central role in the advent of aviation.

Motorless planes can perform two related kinds of flight — gliding and soaring. If you have ever tossed a paper plane into the air and watched it descend you observed gliding flight. In gliding flight a plane descends gradually forward and downward because the force of gravity pulls it earthward while at the same time the wings generate a lifting force to counteract the gravitational pull to buoy up the weight of the craft.

Soaring occurs when a plane in gliding flight encounters air currents that are rising faster than the glider is descending. These sources of lift (air currents) happen at various locations under certain meteorological conditions. Motorless planes or gliders that are specifically designed to soar are called sailplanes. They are to powered airplanes what sailboats are to motorboats.

As long ago as 1799, Sir George Cayley, an English inventor, was experimenting with small kite-like model airplanes made of paper and wood. Later he developed them into large planes that were capable of carrying a human being. Paper planes have continued to be popular ever since and have developed in their own right, increasing in efficiency and maximizing the aerodynamics of small sizes, light weight, and low speed. An example of such a paper glider is the first model in this book, called The Paperwing. **(Paper glider 1, p 10.)**

Full-sized gliders have also evolved from primitive machines in Cayley's day, to sophisticated ones today. There are now scores of different types, classified according to performance level. One class is the Standard Class, of which the Libelle 201 is a good example. This sailplane has been built in greater numbers than any other in that class. **(Paper glider 2, p 14.)**

Gliders are truly fabulous flyers that have chalked up impressive flight records: namely more than 24 hours in the air at one time, over 1000 miles (1600 km) traveled in a single flight, and altitude gains of over 45,000 feet (13,500 m). If you don't have your own full-sized glider you can build a small-scale paper one and perhaps set some records with it. These tiny paper replicas can glide and soar, sometimes remaining airborne for a minute or more, sometimes catching an up-draft and soaring out of sight never to be seen again.

The paper gliders in this book trace the story of motorless flight as the glider developed in design and efficiency. They are modeled on gliders that have a distinctive place in motorless flight history. The planes are made from ordinary index card stock. All can be constructed by anyone having basic craft skills, allowing young and old to experience the thrill of flight firsthand.

NOTE: The proportions of the gliders and sailplanes represented in this book have been slightly altered in the paper models to suit the paper medium, and they are not in scale to each other.

# General assembly instructions for the planes in this book

**If you have not cut paper with a craft knife, begin by making some practice cuts. In pencil draw some squares, triangles, and circles of various sizes on index card stock and cut them out. For straight cuts use a steel edged ruler to guide the knife; make freehand cuts for curved lines. Always cut by drawing the knife towards you and away from the hand used to hold the paper. Continue until you are comfortable with the tools.**

**Use a sharp craft knife (an X-acto knife with a #11 blade) on a suitable cutting surface (an Olfa cutting mat). Practice cutting precisely on the line. Always keep the blade sharp.**

The paper gliders in this book are constructed with three main parts made up of smaller cut out pieces built up in layers: (1) fuselage with vertical stabilizer, (2) wings, and (3) horizontal stabilizer.

**Nothing is cut out of the book.** Instead, make a photocopy of each of the pages containing glider parts. Then, on each photocopy, cut out the center portion (the parts layout). This makes it fit index card stock. Finally tack-glue this portion to card stock and use it as a cutting guide.

Index card tends to curl in one direction. Tack glue the cutting guide to the *convex* side of the card.

Cut through both the tacked on guide paper and the card stock underneath. Remove the part and discard the guide paper. This leaves a clean unmarked glider part, ready for assembly.

For all the cut out pieces, the side that faces up for cutting will be outward or upward facing on the finished glider. This is important for aerodynamic and aesthetic reasons because of the burr on the edges due to cutting.

For assembly, follow the detailed instructions given for each glider type. *Align parts carefully*. Take care to position the bent over parts accurately because they are the fastening tabs for wings and horizontal stabilizer.

GLUING

Stick glue (e.g. Uhu Color Stic), white craft glue, or wood-type model airplane glue can be used. However, it is easier to manage the drying time and reduce warpage with stick glue.

When building up the main parts in layers, apply glue to the entire *smaller* surface to be fastened to a larger one. Press parts firmly together. Continue until the entire main part is done.

Lay the assembled fuselage flat between clean sheets of paper underneath a weight (some heavy books) until the glue is sufficiently set. This will take between 30 and 45 minutes for stick glue, and several hours for white glue.

Discarded remains after the parts have been cut out.

The dihedral angle (upward slanting) of the wings must be adjusted while the parts are being assembled (before the glue is set). Use the angle guide given with each model. If stick glue is used, simply stand the wings on the leading edge (front edge) until the glue has set. If white glue (or model glue) is used, drying the wings is complicated. Some means must be devised to keep each wing from warping while maintaining the dihedral angle.

## ADDING DETAILS

Make the cockpit canopy gray using a felt marker or soft pencil. Make wheels and skids black on gliders that have them. Add other details such as outlines for control surfaces with a soft pencil.

Full-scale gliders are predominantly white because many are of composite construction. Such gliders are heat sensitive, losing structural strength as they become heated.

White reflects the rays of the sun and the gliders remain cool. Gliders made of other materials are also often white to keep them cool because they usually fly where the sun is bright. If you wish to decorate, keep bright colors to a minimum — thin pin stripes, identifying numbers, or perhaps a flag on the tail will suffice for most gliders.

NOTE: It is easier to partially cut out all the pieces first, leaving a small segment of each part attached. Then cut the remaining segments in turn, removing the parts from the card stock. This method of leaving the parts in place gives stability to the sheet while working.

A good work area for model building consists of a large flat surface for spreading things out and plenty of light to see what you are doing. Shown is the proper way to hold knife and paper.

## HOW TO PROCEED

**FIRST, make photocopies**
Make *same-sized* photocopies (100%) of the pages containing the parts for building the paper gliders.

**SECOND, prepare parts sheets**
Cut the **parts layout section** from each photocopy, as indicated on the page, to fit a 5 x 8 inch standard index card. Then tack-glue to the card by applying glue to the areas *between* the parts (**on the backside**) aligning carefully with the edges of the card.

**THIRD, advanced planning**
*Before* beginning to cut out the parts, score those parts that will need to be bent later, and cut opening slits where indicated. Score and cut precisely on the lines.

**FOURTH, cut out the parts**
Cut out each part shown. This must be done carefully, since the success or failure of every other step depends on accurately made parts. *Keep track of the parts by lightly writing the part number in pencil on the backside of each part.*

**FIFTH, build the fuselage**
Begin with the number one fuselage part, adding the other smaller parts on each side to complete the fuselage. Align parts carefully. Add decoration when the glue is dry.

To camber the wings hold between thumb and forefinger of both hands, as shown. Working from the wing root to the wingtip, gently massage the paper to give the upper surface a convex curvature.

### SIXTH, build the wings
Symmetry is essential for wings. Again, align parts carefully. Special care must be taken in those wings consisting of two halves. Temporarily align the halves using masking tape on the bottom side until the joining piece on the topside is glued in place. *The dihedral angle must be set before the glue has dried.* See the dihedral guide for details. Add decoration when the glue is dry.

### SEVENTH, put it all together
Apply glue to the bent-over tabs that join the wings and horizontal stabilizer to the fuselage. Align the wings and stabilizers carefully. Press glued parts together. *Adjust placement carefully, viewing the glider from the top, the front, and the back.* **Symmetry and straight lines in the completed glider are essential**.

Test flights, straight glides, and games such as flying through hoops and spot landings can be done satisfactorily indoors. Catching updrafts for soaring must be done in wide open spaces away from obstacles and traffic.

### EIGHTH, camber the wings
*This is a critical step.* Cambering the wings gives them their ability to generate aerodynamic lift. Holding a wing at the root between thumb and forefinger of both hands, gently massage the paper to give the upper surface a slight convex curvature or camber. Work carefully from the wing root toward the tip and back again. Make sure the left and right wing have the same amount of camber. Avoid kinking the paper. See the instructions for each model for the proper amount of camber.

### NINTH, test fly
This, too, is important. The paper glider must be well trimmed (adjusted) before it can perform satisfactorily. See page 93.

### TENTH, fly for fun
Paper gliders perform best out-of-doors in a light breeze in wide-open spaces, away from obstructions and traffic.

**Caution:
To avoid injury, never fly a paper glider toward another person.**

text continues on page 18 . . .

# The Paperwing

## 1

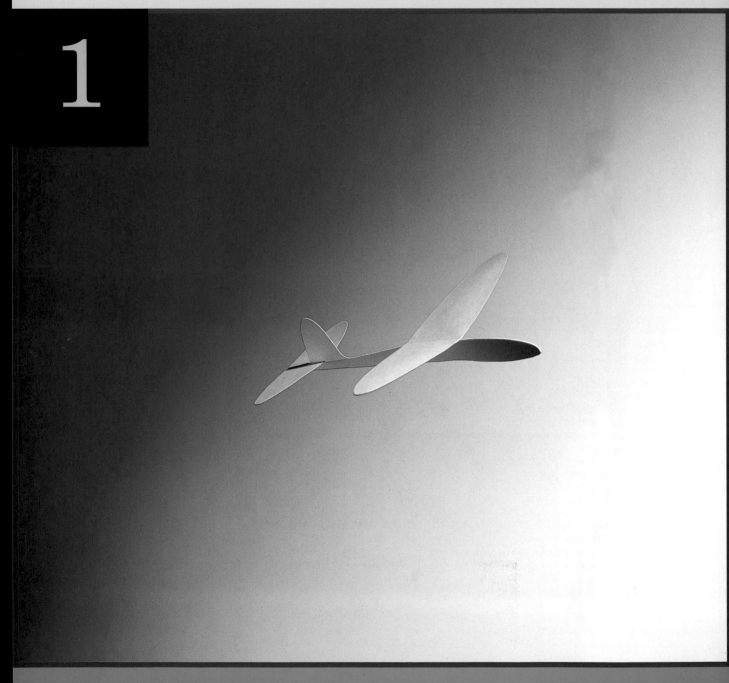

This paper airplane is not modeled after any existing full-sized glider; rather, it is designed as a high performance paper glider. It differs from the other examples in this book (and from full-sized gliders) in how its weight is distributed in relation to the lifting force of the wings. For improved performance, the center of gravity is located near the trailing (back) edge of the wings making the horizontal stabilizer act as a secondary wing. See pp 20-22 for a comparison with other aircraft. **(See text p 5.)**

# Instructions

NOTE: Also refer to general instructions on pp 6-9.

**1** See pages 12 and 13 for this step.

**2** Tack-glue parts cutting guides onto index cards by gluing on the **back-side between the parts**.

**3** Score the fold lines for wing and tail tabs. (After cutting out the pieces, bend tabs outward.)

**4** Cut each piece from the index card stock. Remove light-weight guide paper and discard, leaving a clean unmarked glider part.

NOTE: Cut carefully through both sheets. The cutting side is always the upward or outward facing surface of the finished part.

NOTE: Ensure that the entire contacting surface of a smaller piece being fastened to a larger one is completely covered with glue.

4L
3L
2L
1F
2R
3R
4R

**5** Glue pieces 1F through 4R and 4L to build up fuselage layers, carefully aligning parts.

Press fuselage flat between clean sheets of paper underneath a heavy weight (a few big books) until glue is sufficiently set (about 45 minutes).

**6** Glue 6W to the bottom of wing part 5W.

5W

6W

**9** Camber the wings by curving the paper gently between thumb and foretinger. See below.

7S

NOTE: Make sure wing parts are aligned along the centerline.

The dihedral angle of the wings must be set before the glue dries. See below.

**7** Applying glue to the tail tabs, fasten horizontal stabilizer 10S to the fuselage.

**8** Applying glue to the wing tabs, fasten wing assembly to the fuselage.

Camber:

point of maximum camber, 30% from front

correct

too much

NOTE: After completing the glider, it is important to let the glue set completely (an hour or two) before flying.

Dihedral: 1 in (2.5 cm)

# The Paperwing

## Parts

A

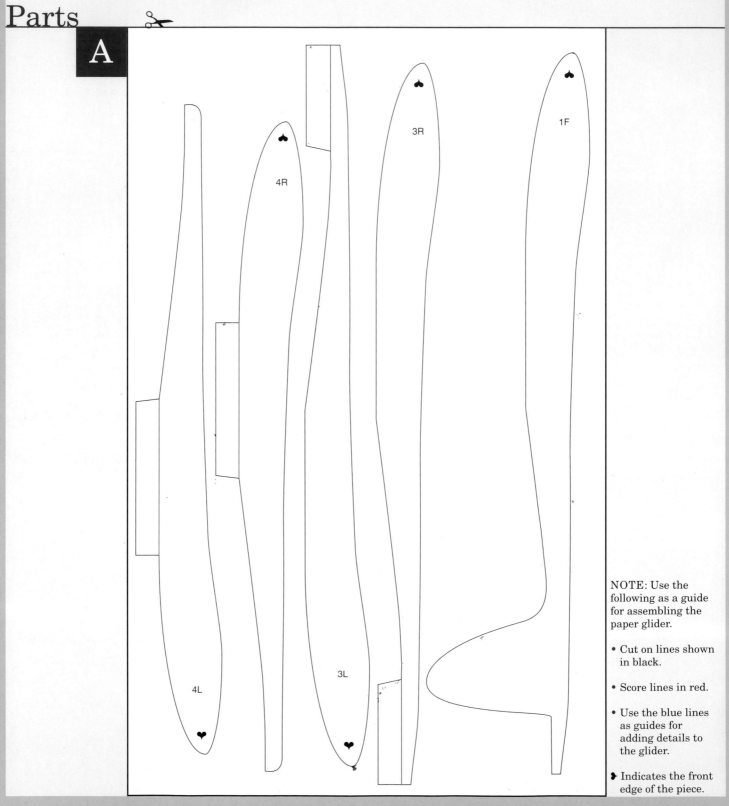

NOTE: Use the following as a guide for assembling the paper glider.

• Cut on lines shown in black.

• Score lines in red.

• Use the blue lines as guides for adding details to the glider.

❥ Indicates the front edge of the piece.

First, photocopy these two pages (100% size). Do not cut the pages from the book .

Then cut out the portion indicated below from the photocopy.
This makes a cutting guide for the various parts and fits a
standard 5 x 8 inch index card. See page 11 for step two.

# Parts

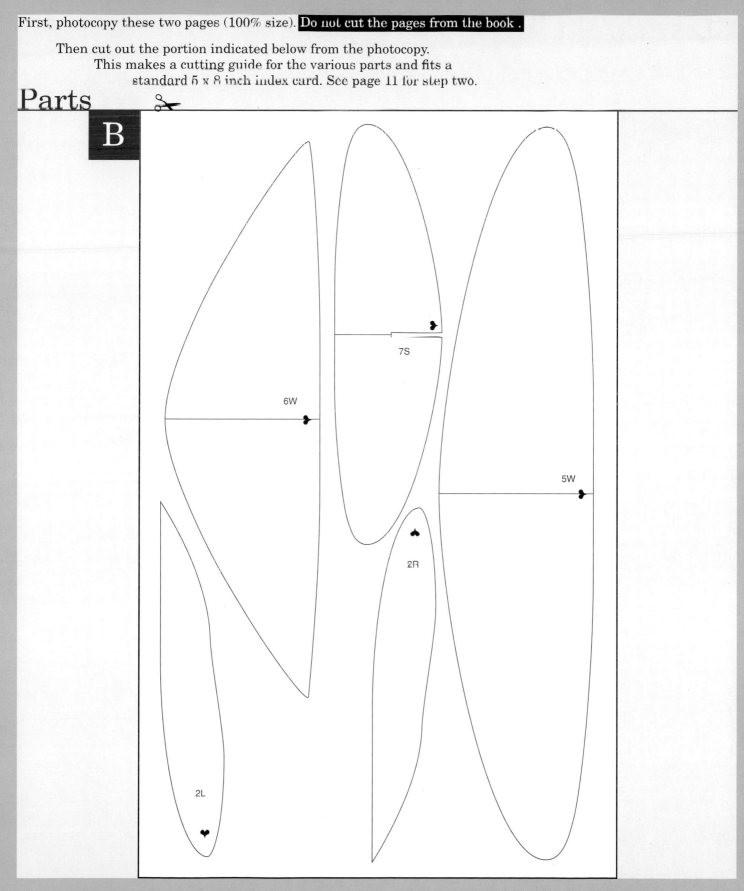

# Glasflügel Libelle 201

## 2

This Standard Class sailplane, of German origin, was designed in 1964 by Eugen Hänle and Wolfgang Hütter. It is among the first all-fibreglass designs. On it pilots immediately set new records, and since then all high-perfomance sailplanes have been constructed of composite materials because of the better streamlining these materials allow. More than 700 Libelles are active worldwide, making it the most numerous model in that class. In 1969 it was voted the world's most beautiful sailplane. **(See text pp 5, 59, 60.)**

# Instructions

NOTE: Also refer to general instructions on pp 6-9.

**1** See pages 16 and 17 for this step.

**2** Tack glue parts cutting guides onto index cards by gluing on the **back-side between the parts**.

**3** Cut opening in fuselage part for horizontal stabilizer.

**5** Cut each piece from the index card stock. Remove light-weight guide paper and discard, leaving a clean unmarked glider part.

**4** Score the fold lines for wing and tail tabs. (After cutting out the pieces, bend tabs outward.)

NOTE: Cut carefully through both sheets. The cutting side is always the upward or outward facing surface of the finished part.

NOTE: Ensure that the entire contacting surface of a smaller piece being fastened to a larger one is completely covered with glue

**6** Glue pieces 1F through 5R and 5L to build up fuselage layers, carefully aligning parts.

Press fuselage flat between clean sheets of paper underneath a heavy weight (a few big books) until glue is sufficiently set (about 45 minutes).

**7** Bring wing parts 6R and 6L together, fastening with 7T. Then glue 8R and 8L to the bottom of the wing. Finally glue 9B to the very bottom.

**8** Applying glue to the tail tabs, fasten horizontal stabilizer 10S to the fuselage.

**10** Camber the wings by curving the paper gently between thumb and forefinger. See below.

NOTE: Make sure wing parts are aligned along the centerline.

The dihedral angle of the wings must be set before the glue dries. See below.

**9** Applying glue to the wing tabs, fasten wing assembly to the fuselage.

Camber:

point of maximum camber, 30% from front

correct

too much

Dihedral: 1 1/2 in (3.75 cm)

NOTE: After completing the glider, it is important to let the glue set completely (an hour or two) before flying.

# Glasflügel Libelle 201

## Parts

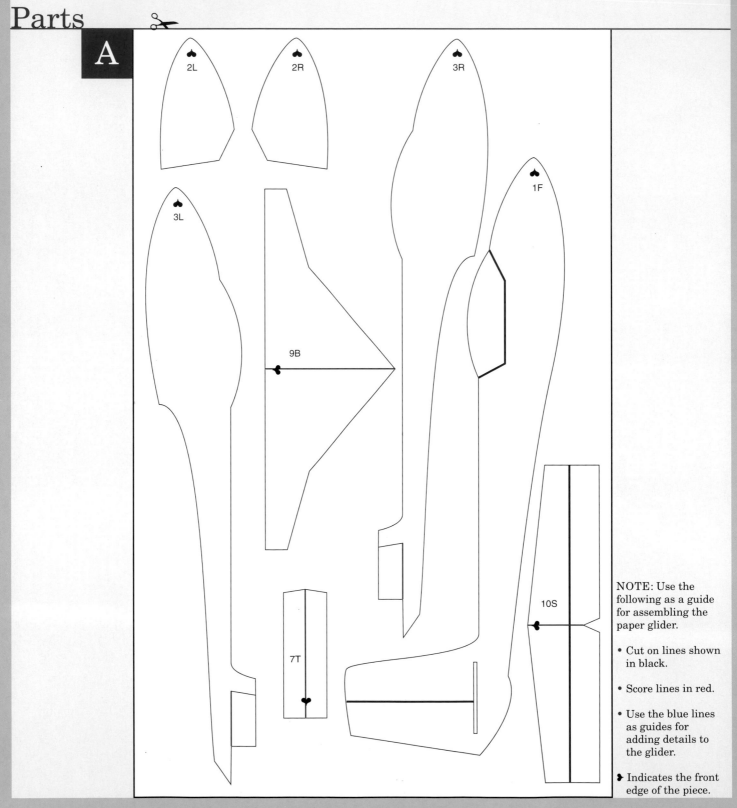

A

NOTE: Use the following as a guide for assembling the paper glider.

• Cut on lines shown in black.

• Score lines in red.

• Use the blue lines as guides for adding details to the glider.

➤ Indicates the front edge of the piece.

First, photocopy these two pages (100% size).

Then cut out the portion indicated below from the photocopy.
This makes a cutting guide for the various parts and fits a
standard 5 x 8 inch index card. See page 15 for step two.

# Parts ✂

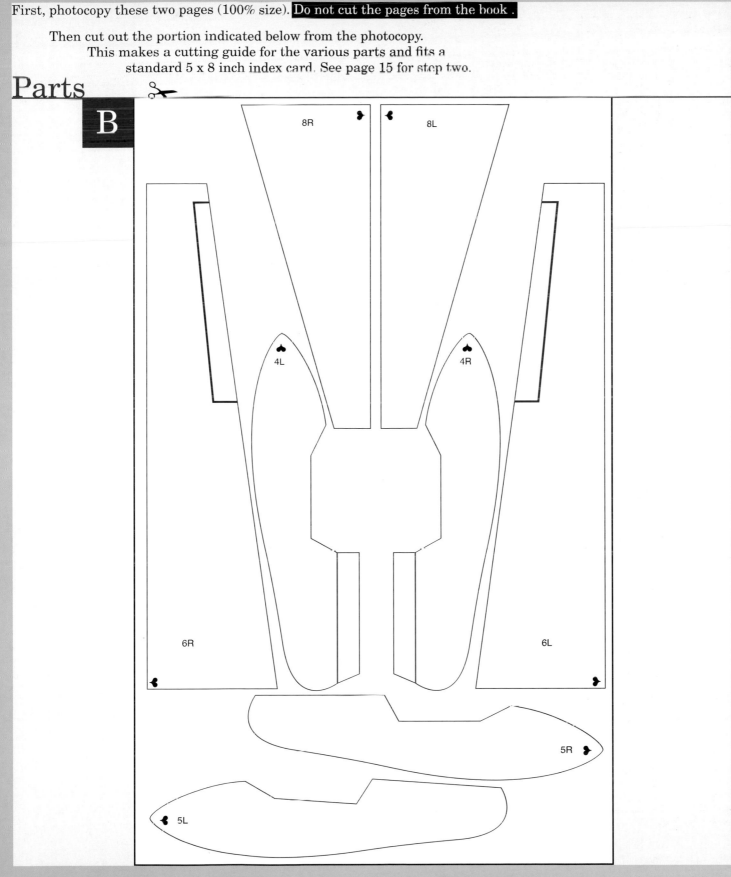

**I**NVENTORS in ancient times, inspired by birds flying overhead, built the first flying machines — tethered kites. Free-flight was not so easily achieved. Since aerodynamic principles were unknown, the similarities between a kite flying on a string and a bird flying freely were not recognized. It was assumed that wing flapping was necessary to remain airborne. This idea was further reinforced by the fact that the similar action of rowing a boat in water worked very well. But had people paid more attention to hawks, eagles, and gulls, soaring overhead without so much as a single wingbeat, free-flight might have occurred much sooner than it did. It took many hundreds of years before anyone seriously looked to the soaring birds for clues.

In the 1500s Leonardo da Vinci made a modest beginning. He realized correctly that for successful flight it was the shape of the device flown that determined how the resisting force of moving air could be harnessed and controlled. However, even Leonardo did not understand that bird wings produce two independent forces — one for remaining airborne and the other for propulsion, and that flapping is involved only in the latter. Real progress did not occur for another 300 years when the basic principles of fluid dynamics were better understood; when in the mid-1700s, Swiss mathematician, Daniel Bernoulli, discovered that the pressure of a fluid always decreases as its rate of flow is increased (Bernoulli's Principle).

This law of nature explained that the same properties kept a bird, a kite, or an aircraft aloft. See figures 1 and 2.

In 1799 the Englishman, Sir George Cayley, experimenting with kites, was the first person to understand the separateness of the force of lift from thrust, and the application of aerodynamic principles. Cayley understood that controlling differential air pressure was the key to generating a lifting force and made careful studies of the ratio between wing shape and surface area to lifting capacity. He also undertood how the addition of smaller surfaces, strategically located, gave stability. Cayley knew about the importance of adjusting surfaces to correct angles (called the angle of attack) relative to the airflow for balancing the various forces at play. He began by utilizing two arch top kites (a large one for producing lift and a smaller one for stability) combined into a single device.

Cayley was the first person to fly successfully many different kinds of small-scale wood and paper models. After 1806 he built machines with increasingly larger wing areas that could carry weights up to 80 or 90 pounds (36-41 kg). Cayley had replaced the smaller kite used for stability with a tail, introducing for the first time the concept of horizontal and vertical stabilizing surfaces. But these gliders could not be adjusted while in flight. They had to be trimmed for level flight before they were launched. Once airborne they could fly only straight ahead and were at the mercy of any fluctuations in air currents.

## Figure 1

Demonstrating Bernoulli's Principle

Hold the narrow edge of a lightweight piece of writing paper (approximately 3 x 8 in or 7.5 x 20 cm) between thumb and forefinger, letting the free end droop. Then blow over your thumb and along the paper. If done correctly the drooping end should rise because the moving air exerts less pressure downward than the still air beneath does upward. Consequently the air beneath pushes the paper upward. A lifting force has been created.

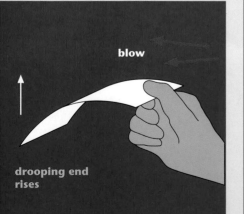

blow

drooping end
rises

## Figure 2
How a wing creates lift

A wing increases the speed of the airflow over its upper surface so that pressure in this area is reduced. This is accomplished by making the upper wing surface curved — called camber. The distance from front to back along the curved surface is greater than along the straight lower one. Because the molecules flowing along the curve have farther to travel than the ones beneath, they increase their speed and become spaced farther apart in order to resume their former position when they leave the wing at the trailing edge. This faster moving air exerts less pressure, which means that a partial vacuum is created above the wing — suction. (By the application of Bernoulli's Principle.) The now higher pressure beneath pushes the wing upward into the vacuum, creating a lifting force. This lift acts through a point about one third of the distance between the leading and trailing edges of a wing, the point of maximum camber.

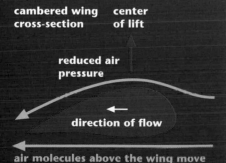

**cambered wing cross-section**  **center of lift**

**reduced air pressure**

**direction of flow**

air molecules above the wing move faster, are spaced farther apart, and therefore have less pressure (suction), allowing the pressure underneath to push the wing into the vacuum — lift

Because of his many successful unmanned flights, in 1853 Cayley sent his coachman for a straight descending glide from a higher point to a lower one on his largest machine. It became the first observed and recorded occurrence of a human being in free-flight. For his work, Cayley earned the title of Father of Aviation. His work encouraged others to follow, but successful controlled flight eluded most of the early pioneers.

In Germany, however, Otto Lilienthal, a marine engineer, made real progress. After some twenty years of observing seagulls in flight and studying bird anatomy, in 1889 he published his *Der Vogel Flug als Grundlage der Fliegekunst* (Bird-flight as the basis for the Art of Flying).

For the first time someone was taking a new approach to the problems of flight by seriously studying birds, not for their wing flapping but for their gliding flight. The following year he built his first flying machine, modeled on his observations. Piloting — controlling the man-made "birds" while in flight — became one of his main objectives. He understood that the lifting force produced by the curvature of the feathers was improved by the fact that bird wings are longer than they are wide. Air resistance relative to the lifting force was less. Also, he saw that gulls make slight adjustments in the positions and angles of their wings and tails to balance themselves in gliding flight. Piloting therefore meant balancing the various forces at work as demanded by the fluctuations in air currents encountered while flying.

As a result of these observations the gliders he built assumed a bird-like shape, and the pilot moved his body about in flight to alter the relationship between the center of gravity and the lifting force of the wings. Lilienthal had invented the hang glider. **(Paper glider 3, p 28.)**

In the next five years Lilienthal made over 2000 successful gliding flights using weight shifting for balance, some covering distances of nearly 1000 feet (300 m). This method of maintaining equilibrium, however, has limitations. Rather than initiating guidance to the machine in a positive manner, weight shifting is always compensatory, the pilot reacting to the aircraft's movement in any direction. If a misjudgement is made in the position of the pilot's body, or unexpected gusts occur, the machine can become dangerously unstable. Weight shifting also limits the size of aircraft that can be successfully balanced to rather small and lightweight machines.

Unfortunately Lilienthal's calculations for wing size, lift, and air resistance were not very accurate. On August 9, 1896 his glider pitched up in a gust. He was unable to compensate by weight shifting and the craft stalled, pitched nose-down, and crashed. Lilienthal died from the injuries he sustained. But he had gained the reputation of being the first true pilot.

**F**LIGHT involves the creation of two forces by artificial means to oppose two forces occuring naturally — the force of lift must be created to counteract the earth's gravity, and the force of thrust to oppose air resistance.

## GRAVITY AND LIFT

To work, aircraft wings must alter air pressure. They do this in two ways. First, as they move forward they slice the surrounding air into two layers, one above and one beneath the wings. Both layers are made up of the same number of molecules. If the wing has a curved upper surface, the molecules moving across the top surface have farther to travel than the ones underneath. As they try to maintain their position in relation to the rest of the air molecules, they become spaced farther apart and their speed increases so that when they reach the back edge of the wing, they again match their position with the lower molecules. In accordance with Bernoulli's Principle, the faster moving and more widely spaced molecules exert less pressure downward than the slower moving and more closely spaced lower molecules do upward, creating a pressure differential. The reduced pressure above the wings creates suction, much like a vacuum cleaner does. The air underneath pushes the wing into the area of reduced pressure, and the aircraft is buoyed up as it moves forward, counteracting gravity. (See figure 2, p 19).

Second, if the leading edge of the wings is raised slightly, allowing air molecules to strike the slanted lower surface, the amount of lift generated can be increased. This slanting is called the *angle of attack*. See figure 3. However, if this angle is too great lift stops because air no longer flows smoothly over the upper surface disrupting the suction and the wing *stalls*. See figure 4.

## DRAG AND THRUST

Lift is possible only by forward motion. As a glider moves forward air molecules are pushed aside causing a certain amount of resistance. On the one hand this resistance turns into the pressure that makes lift possible, on the other hand, it becomes drag, which slows a glider down. The resistance of air molecules being disturbed by forward motion is called *pressure drag*.

## Figure 3
Increasing the lifting force

The lifting force created by a wing through reduced air pressure over the upper surface (suction) can be increased if the leading edge of the wing is raised slightly. This incline is called the angle of attack. It allows the airflow to strike the lower surface. As air is deflected downward, it provides a force in the opposite direction. This additional pressure beneath the wings increases the overall lifting force. Even a flat uncambered wing can generate lift just by having an angle of attack, as is the case in some kites. Over the years many different cambered wing shapes have been used on various aircraft. Powered aircraft that are designed to fly at very high speeds have thin wings with only slight camber. Glider wings have generous camber and are designed to produce the maximum amount of lift with a minimum penalty of drag at moderate speeds. Every wing design of any particular cross-section shape has a best angle of attack.

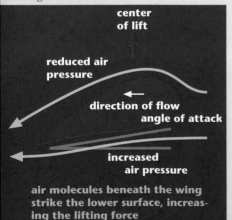

center of lift

reduced air pressure

direction of flow
angle of attack

increased air pressure

air molecules beneath the wing strike the lower surface, increasing the lifting force

## Figure 4
Stall — if the angle of attack is too great the wing no longer produces lift

Lift stops if the angle of attack exceeds about 15 degrees because the air flowing over the upper surface, unable to follow the steep curve, separates and breaks into eddies. Then the air striking the lower surface creates a backward instead of upward force (drag).

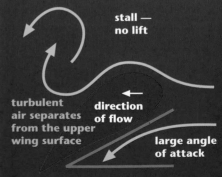

stall — no lift

turbulent air separates from the upper wing surface

direction of flow

large angle of attack

air molecules striking the lower surface create a backward instead of upward force

## Figure 5

Drag — the resisting force of air
Thrust — a propelling force

Once launched, the force of gravity propels a glider through the air. This is called thrust. The steeper a plane's gliding angle the greater this force becomes, making the glider fly faster. But air resists being disturbed. This is called drag. It slows a glider down and its force increases with speed. Drag and thrust counteract each other.

There are three kinds of drag: pressure drag, induced drag, and frictional drag. These combine to make up the overall drag acting on an aircraft in flight. Pressure drag is the general resistance of air to disturbance. This is what you feel when you wave your arm or run. The bigger the frontal area of an object, the greater this drag. Air always flows from an area of high pressure to an area of low pressure: therefore, in the process of generating lift, air slips around the wingtips creating a vortex. This is induced drag. Because of the relative stickiness of air, any surface of the aircraft over which air flows creates frictional drag.

Excessive drag is the bane of gliders, and reducing it has been a major objective in sailplane design.

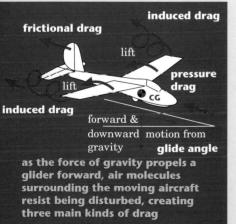

**frictional drag** **induced drag**
lift
**pressure drag**
lift
CG
**induced drag**
forward & downward motion from gravity **glide angle**

as the force of gravity propels a glider forward, air molecules surrounding the moving aircraft resist being disturbed, creating three main kinds of drag

This drag increases as a glider's speed increases. Furthermore, any surfaces on an airplane not parallel to the airflow add to this drag, including a wing's angle of attack and stabilizers adjusted to maintain straight and level flight.

Additionally, the pressure differential above and beneath a wing creates a vortex as air slips around the wingtip from the area of high pressure to that of low pressure. This turbulence, which always accompanies lift production, is called *induced drag*.

Air molecules flowing over an object also tend to stick to the object's surface, adding to the air's resistance — called *frictional drag*. The smaller the object and the slower it moves the greater the frictional drag. In fact, for a small flying insect, the air seems as thick and gooey as swimming in syrup would be to us.

The various types of drag combine into a single force as the glider moves forward through the air.

The presence of drag demands that a glider have a constant thrusting force to remain in motion. This is obtained by designing the glider so that the center of gravity (CG) — the point where the glider's weight appears to be concentrated — is slightly ahead of the point where the lifting force of the wings buoys up the glider (the center of lift). Because the glider's weight is thus concentrated in its nose, the force of gravity automatically moves the glider in both a forward and downward direction. See figure 5.

## BALANCE AND STABILITY

The degree of stability inherent in an aircraft depends on its overall design. As Lilienthal had discovered, all aircraft in flight tend to be unstable in three ways: they roll left or right along a longitudinal axis, pitch nose up or down along a lateral axis running through the wings, and yaw from side to side around a vertical axis. The axes

## Figure 6

Dihedral angle

The wings on most aircraft angle upward away from the fuselage. This gives roll stability. In level flight each wing produces the same amount of lift. When an aircraft with dihedral is banked, as when upset by a gust of wind, the downgoing wing's exposed surface lengthens and its lift consequently increases, while the upgoing wing's exposed area shortens and its lift decreases. This lift differential causes an opposite rolling force and the plane rights itself, restoring equilibrium. The greater the dihedral angle the more stable the airplane.

Paper gliders require a dihedral angle somewhat greater than full sized planes because their very light weight makes them susceptible to upset by even light gusts of wind.

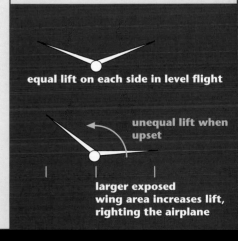

**equal lift on each side in level flight**

**unequal lift when upset**

**larger exposed wing area increases lift, righting the airplane**

## Figure 7

**Three-axis control in a standard aircraft**

An aircraft in flight can rotate about its center of gravity along three axes. (1) Its rolling motion is controlled by ailerons in the wings. (2) Pitch is controlled by an elevator in the horizontal stabilizer. (3) Yaw is controlled by a rudder in the vertical stabilizer. These are small flaps on the trailing edges that swing back and forth like a door on its hinges. When operated in harmony, these controls provide equilibrium in flight — three-axis control.

The ailerons move differentially, when one is moved up the other goes down, and vice versa, creating a difference in lift between the two wings — down, and lift is increased; up, and it is decreased. This makes the aircraft bank and turn to left or right.

By moving up or down, the elevator contols the air flowing over the horizontal stabilizer. When it is raised the pressure over the upper surface of the stabilizer increases, pushing downward, which pitches the nose up as the plane rotates about the center of gravity.

The rudder swings to left or right and keeps the aircraft pointing straight into the airflow during flight.

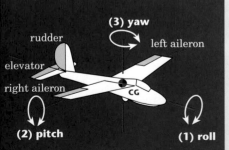

**while in flight, the elevator, ailerons, and rudder allow for equilibrium to be maintained, as well as giving directional control for maneuvering the aircraft**

intersect at the center of gravity. This means that an aircraft pivots freely about its center of gravity, and this movement must be stabilized for steady flight. Since Cayley's day it has been known that this can be accomplished by having both vertical and horizontal stabilizers and wings that slant upward slightly away from the fuselage (a dihedral angle). See figure 6.

Any upset by a gust of wind or turbulent air needs to be immediately corrected if steady flight is to be maintained. Therefore, besides having horizontal and vertical stabilizing surfaces, small moveable surfaces are required so that the pilot can make immediate adjustments to maintain equilibrium. These control surfaces must be large enough to also provide directional control for maneuvering the aircraft. See figure 7.

Neither Cayley nor Lilienthal had discoverd how moveable control surfaces could be added because the mechanisms required are complicated.

## GLIDER PERFORMANCE

A glider's loss of height as gravity pulls it downward and forward is called sink. Every glider has a particular *rate of sink*, measured in units per minute. The amount of sink in relation to a glider's forward movement, is known as the *glide ratio*. At a constant airspeed the ratio of the lifting force of the wings and the resistant force of drag is exactly equal to the glide ratio. Therefore for a glider to have a high glide ratio, drag must be kept at a minimum. See figure 8.

Dividing the weight of a glider by the surface area of its wings is a ratio known as *wing loading*. The lighter the wing loading the smaller the sink rate, and the longer a glider will remain aloft in still air. It "floats." Gliders with very light wing loadings have limited usefulness. They are at the mercy of turbulence. For operation in the varied conditions found in the atmosphere greater wing loadings are needed to give higher airspeed and greater stability in rough air. This discovery in the 1920s was a major advance in soaring. Because of their light weight, paper gliders are all "floaters," especially the first model in this book, which is of non-conventional configuration.

Proper elevator adjustment is important to maximize performance in gliding flight. In aircraft of conventional configuration the horizontal stabilizer and the elevator provide a counterbalancing force compensating for the automatic downward pitching motion due to the center of gravity's location ahead of the center of lift. Furthermore, in all gliding flight, controlling pitch is especially important because it also controls airspeed. Airspeed, in turn, affects the glide ratio and overall performance of the glider. Every glider has an optimum speed for a best glide ratio. This is its cruising speed. Adjusting a glider to fly at this speed is called *trimming for cruise*. See figure 9.

Cayley and Lilienthal had only limited success in maintaining a plane's equilibrium. Their gliders were not maneuverable. For this a new design was needed.

## Figure 8

Glider performance

If a glider produces a lot of drag in relation to the lifting force of its wings, it must descend rapidly to the ground in order for the force of gravity to maintain adequate forward momentum. It has a steep glide angle, and thus a poor glide ratio because it cannot travel very far before it lands. On the other hand, a glider producing little drag in relation to the lifting force of its wings flies with a shallower glide angle and can fly much farther. It has a high glide ratio. The relationship between the amount of lift that a wing produces and its accompanying drag at a particular speed is exactly the same ratio as that between a glider's height and its glide distance. That is, the lift to drag ratio and the glide ratio are identical.

If a wing has a lift to drag ratio of 30:1, that number is also the glider's glide ratio. In practical terms it means that for roughly every 5000 feet of altitude it can travel thirty miles.

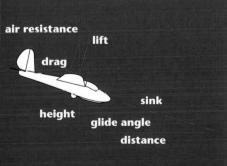

the lift to drag ratio and the glide ratio (height to distance) are identical

ILIENTHAL'S records became the basis for the work of Wilbur and Orville Wright, two American bicycle builders who turned their attention to airplanes. They began their work with the newly-invented box kite. They made detailed observations of aerodynamic properties and applied new findings carefully. To aid in their work they constructed a wind tunnel in which conditions could be controlled for observation. In it they tested small models.

Their full-sized models were tested at Kitty Hawk, in North Carolina. First they made tethered flights, then proceeded to free-flight, and by the end of 1900, they had made their first successful manned gliding flights.

On their machines the pilot worked hand and foot operated moveable surfaces to achieve stability in three axes — the wingtips were differentially twisted to control roll, the elevator in the horizontal stabilizer controlled pitch, and the rudder in the tail controlled yaw. This gave them sufficient control to maintain stability in rough as well as smooth air, and provided directional control for maneuvering the glider.

Three-axis control was the Wright brothers' first and greatest contribution to aeronautics. It has become standardized, with variations, in all aircraft except hang gliders, where weight shifting is still utilized. See figure 7.

The Wrights next addressed regular sustained flight. For this they would need a means of propulsion. Steam engines had been tried but were too heavy. The Wright brothers recog-

nized the potential of Gottlieb Daimler and Karl Benz's gasoline burning internal combustion engine, and set about designing a small lightweight version of their own. When fitted to their airplane it

## Figure 9

Performance and speed

In motorless aircraft, airspeed is controlled solely by altering pitch. This is done by adjusting the elevator. In a glider of ordinary design the center of gravity is located ahead of the center of lift. This configuration allows a slightly raised elevator (positive trim) to pitch the nose up a little, causing the glider to fly with a particular angle of attack. Increase the pitch and the glider flies at a slower speed. Decrease it and speed increases.

Every wing is most efficient at a particular angle of attack and speed. This speed must be maintained for a best glide ratio. Therefore a certain amount of positive trim is always necessary to maintain a proper flight attitude. Positive trim also helps in maintaining balance despite any air turbulence. Gliders that have a best glide ratio at higher speeds are better able to penetrate rough air.

Given the comparative lightness of gliders, the location of the CG relative to the center of lift is critical for correctly counterbalancing weight (acting through the CG) by elevator trim to achieve good performance. In most gliders the speed range for maximum performance is quite narrow.

with elevator raised, airflow is deflected upward, increasing pressure above the horizontal stabilizer

the tail is pushed downward and the nose pitches up

CG ahead of lift

the location of the center of gravity, relative to the wing's lift, is important for proper pitch trim and good glide performance proved to have just the right ratio of power to weight to get the craft off the ground. Thus in 1903 the era of powered flight began. The thrusting force that the wing flapping of birds provides was successfully emulated by the spinning propeller. This is the second contribution the Wrights made to aviation.

In 1911 Orville Wright returned to Kitty Hawk for further experiments to learn something about soaring flight and to take advantage of the rising air currents and remain aloft without an artificial source of power. Orville was accompanied by Alec Ogilvie, a fellow aviation pioneer from Britain. They modified the Wright glider no. 5 by lengthening the fuselage, adding a forward boom that carried a sandbag as ballast, and adding supplementary stabilizers. The success of their flights in this modified glider was remarkable. Orville describes the event:

*In 1911 Mr. Alec Ogilvie and I continued the soaring experiments at Kitty Hawk and succeeded in making a number of flights of more than five minutes duration (the longest of which was nine and three-quarters minutes) without loss of any height at all. In many cases we landed at a higher point than the one from which we started. I see no reason why flights of several hours duration cannot be made without the use of a motor. But, of course, these flights must be made in rising trends of air — a condition required by all birds for soaring flight.*

This event marked the first recorded human soaring flight. For the first time humans could do what the soaring birds did. This is the third contribution the Wrights made to aviation. Henceforth aircraft development would be along two distinct lines — powered and motorless.

Orville Wright soars the Wright Glider no. 5 over the sand dunes of Kitty Hawk, making the world's first sustained motorless flight.

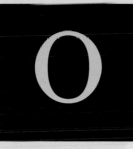

**O**RVILLE'S success at soaring stimulated great enthusiasm and began a grassroots movement of gliding experiments. But the war in Europe in 1914, forced everyone involved in aviation to divert their attention from motorless flight to perfecting the powered airplane as a weapon of war.

When the war ended in 1918 Americans began to develop the powered airplane that had great military and commercial potential, which they rapidly exploited. Germany, which was forbidden by the Treaty of Versailles to develop aircraft for military use, turned to gliders. No powered aircraft could be built. Germany's engineers, scientists, and aviation enthusiasts pursued gliding flight with a passion, and it became an official technical subject in universities.

A magazine, *Flugsport* (Sport Aviation), emphasized the sporting potential of soaring flight, and widely popularized the activity. In 1919 the first soaring meet was held at the Wasserkuppe in the Rhoen mountain range of central Germany, an ideal site with smooth slopes for launching gliders as well as ridges for producing rising currents of air.

The next year, 1920, the meet became an official competition, setting the stage for what has come to characterize the world of soaring flight — achieving goals and setting records. This first official soaring competition produced a winning flight of 2 minutes 23 seconds, achieved by Wolfgang Klemperer.

In the 1921 meet, Klemperer made some significant improvements to his glider and achieved a 13 minute flight. Orville's record had fallen.

For this meet, for the first time, a system of "A" "B" and "C" achievement badges was established, and Klemperer's was the first "C" badge given. ("C" designated a flight of 5 minutes duration. The "A" and "B" badges were given for piloting proficiency.)

The next day, a student named Martens, broke Klemperer's record with a 15 minute flight, and later another student, named Harth, made a 21 minute flight, more than doubling Orville's time. He achieved the third "C" badge in the world.

This systematic marking of soaring achievements is still in place today, and all soaring pilots participate in it. The "A" badge now designates solo flight, "B" the first solo soaring flight, "C" one hour of soaring flight, and so on, including not only duration but also distances covered, speeds attained, altitudes gained, and various combinations of achievements in "silver," "gold," and "diamond" catagories.

In 1922 national meets were also held in Britain and France, beginning a trend that continues to this day, when many countries around the world hold annual national soaring competitions.

In England, a French pilot named Manyrolle raised the record time considerably with a flight of 3 hours 20 minutes. Orville's prediction of prolonged motorless flight had been realized.

Gliders of every description were being built. According to a U.S. pilot and military observer named Allen, the gliders of the day could be put into four classes of machines: (1) sailplanes, gliders with improved performance, (2) hang gliders, primitive machines having weight-shifting control, (3) powerplanes with engines removed, and (4) freaks of all kinds, built by non-technical enthusiasts.

Gliders were launched down a slope using an elastic shock cord. Either a number of people or horses were used to stretch the cord while the glider was held fast. Once the cord was fully extended the glider was released and catapulted into the air.

At that time the goal of soaring was duration flying. The source of lift was the band of air forced upward as wind strikes rising ground called *ridge lift*, which the Wrights had also used. Because the gliders didn't go anywhere, most designers concentrated on the lightness of their craft, slow air speed, and a low sink rate, which they thought would keep them aloft the longest. See figure 10.

German designers had other ideas. They built sailplanes that were heavier with higher wing loadings, had increased air speeds, higher aspect ratios with greater lift-to-drag ratios, making them less susceptible to upsets in gusty conditions and better able to penetrate rough air. In such machines pilots could venture outside the sources of lift and fly from place to place away from the ridges.

Through consistent and organized effort, after the first world war, they had moved far ahead of the rest of the world in several ways: developing the performance levels of sailplanes, gaining an understanding of meteorological conditions, and refining soaring techniques to suit different conditions.

In the United States at this time most aviation remained largely a military affair. But it was brought sharply into the American public mind in 1927 when Charles Lindbergh made his dramatic trans-Atlantic solo flight. North Americans became "air minded."

Popular scientific magazines advertised blueprints, of German origin, that could be ordered for the home building of primary gliders. These consisted of open-frame fuselages with the pilot seated unenclosed in the nose, with wings and stabilizers supported by wire braces. They made aviation available to an eager public. **(Paper glider 4, p 32.)**

Meanwhile, Wasserkuppe had become a soaring mecca for testing new designs and flight duration challenges. Schools were established in Germany and other parts of Europe and the U.S. for proper flight training. A gliding school was established in 1928 at Cape Cod, Massachusetts, where Ralph Barnaby achieved the first American "C" badge with a flight of 15 minutes. Soon thereafter Peter Hesselbach, the school's chief pilot, set an American record with a flight of over 4 hours.

In 1929 Hawley Bowlus in the U.S. built a high-performance sailplane, known as the *Paperwing*. It was so named because ordinary butcher

## Figure 10
Soaring flight in ridge lift

When wind blows against ground that is rising, air is deflected upward. Gliders can fly back and forth in this band of rising air along the crest of the ridge and remain airborne as long as this air is rising as fast as or faster than the glider's sink rate.

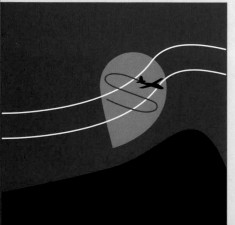

paper was used in its construction. In this plane he pushed the American soaring record to almost 9 hours. But most American gliding flights at that time, were measured, not even in minutes, but in seconds.

More enthusiasm for gliding in the U.S. occurred during the depression which began in 1929. Dwindling resources forced many aviation enthusiasts to give up powered flight. To remain active in aviation they turned to gliding, which was less costly. And as sales of powered aircraft decreased, established airplane manufacturers turned to building primary gliders, which they sold at very low cost. As a result, for the first time, factory built gliders were widely available in the U.S.

In 1928 Edward Evans, financier and director of the Aviation Bureau of the Detroit Board of Commerce, began a gliding club. Before long this club's mandate was broadened to become the National Glider Association, encouraging many other clubs to form. But the pilots remained largely untrained and there were many crashes.

In 1930 Elmira, New York was chosen by the NGA for the first American National glider meet. It was ideal for generating updrafts in wind blowing in almost any direction, and the valleys below had many ideal landing fields. On the very first flight there, Jack O'Meara logged 1 hour 34 minutes. With this site, soaring in the United States became solidly established. The National Soaring Museum is located there.

NATIONAL SOARING MUSEUM

Charles Lindbergh preparing for launch in a Bowlus Paperwing, 1930.

text continues on page 36 . . .

# Lilienthal 1895 Glider

**3**

Otto Lilienthal observed birds in flight and studied their anatomy before he built his first glider in 1890. His bird-like machine was a hang glider, on which the pilot hung from a harness inside a hoop and shifted his weight — forward and backward or side to side — to maintain flight equilibrium. Over the next few years he built various models of hang gliders, some of which were biplanes. **(See text p 19.)**

# Instructions

NOTE: Also refer to general instructions on pp 6-9.

**1** See pages 30 and 31 for this step.

**2** Tack-glue parts cutting guides onto index cards by gluing on the **back-side between the parts.**

**3** Cut openings in fuselage and wings for horizontal stabilizer and pilot.

**4** Score the fold lines for wing and tail tabs. (After cutting out the pieces, bend tabs outward.)

**5** Cut each piece from the index card stock. Remove light-weight guide paper and discard, leaving a clean unmarked glider part.

NOTE: Cut carefully through both sheets. The cutting side is always the upward or outward facing surface of the finished part.

**6** Glue pieces 1F through 9R and 9L to build up fuselage layers, carefully aligning parts.

NOTE: Ensure that the entire contacting surface of a smaller piece being fastened to a larger one is completely covered with glue.

Press fuselage flat between clean sheets of paper underneath a heavy weight (a few big books) until glue is sufficiently set (about 45 minutes).

**7** Glue 11B to the bottom of wing part 10W.

10W

11B

NOTE: Make sure wing parts are aligned along the centerline.

The dihedral angle of the wings must be set before the glue dries. See below.

**8** Applying glue to the tail tabs, fasten horizontal stabilizer 12S to the fuselage.

12S

**9** Applying glue to the wing tabs, fasten wing assembly to the fuselage. Pilot goes through wing slot.

**10** Camber the wings by curving the paper gently between thumb and forefinger. See below.

point of maximum camber, 30% from front

Camber:

correct

too much

$^1/_2$ in (1.25 cm)

NOTE: After completing the glider, it is important to let the glue set completely (an hour or two) before flying.

# Lilienthal 1895 Glider

## Parts

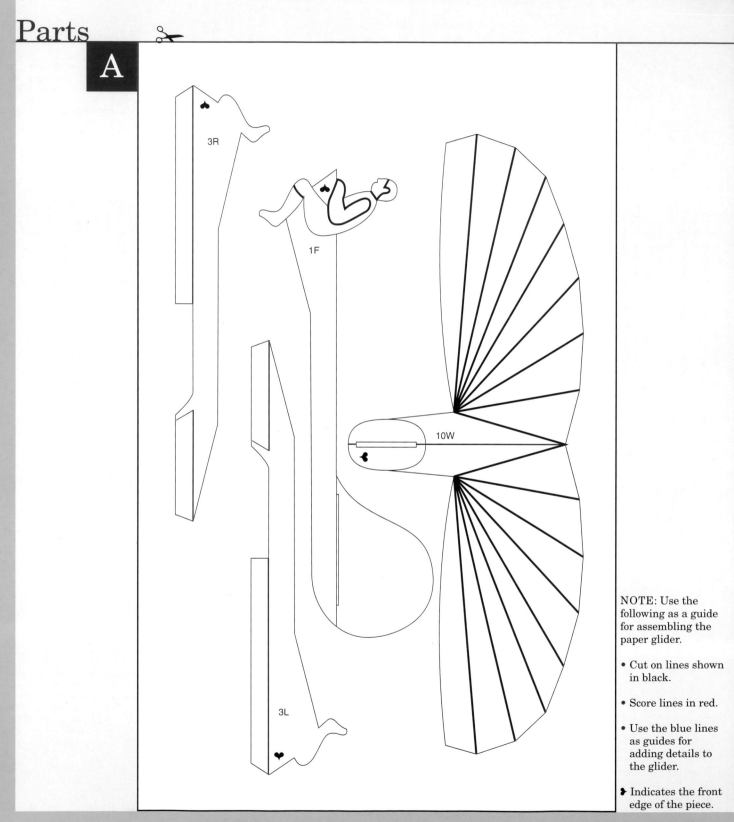

3R

1F

10W

3L

NOTE: Use the following as a guide for assembling the paper glider.

- Cut on lines shown in black.

- Score lines in red.

- Use the blue lines as guides for adding details to the glider.

➔ Indicates the front edge of the piece.

First, photocopy these two pages (100% size).

Then cut out the portion indicated below from the photocopy.
This makes a cutting guide for the various parts and fits a
standard 5 x 8 inch index card. See page 29 for step two.

# Parts

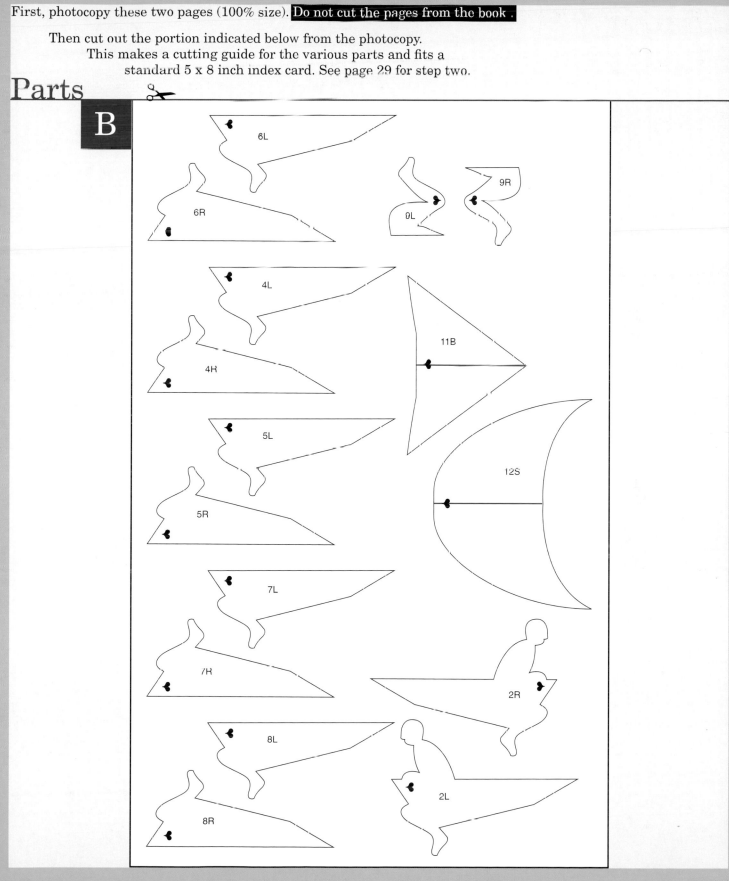

# Primary Glider

4

In the 1930s mail order blueprints for home building open-framed gliders — called primary gliders — having wire-braced fabric-covered wings and stabilizers, were advertised extensively in popular scientific magazines. Anyone handy with basic tools could build one in the home workshop. Later they were also factory built. These primitive machines played an important role in introducing gliding to the public. **(See text p 26.)**

# Instructions

NOTE: Also refer to general instructions on pp 6-9.

**1** See pages 34 and 35 for this step.

**2** Tack-glue parts cutting guides onto index cards by gluing on the **back-side between the parts**.

**4** Cut each piece from the index card stock. Remove light-weight guide paper and discard, leaving a clean unmarked glider part.

**3** Score the fold lines for wing and tail tabs. (After cutting out the pieces, bend tabs outward.)

**5** Glue pieces 1F through 9R and 9L to build up fuselage layers, carefully aligning parts.

NOTE: Cut carefully through both sheets. The cutting side is always the upward or outward facing surface of the finished part.

NOTE: Ensure that the entire contacting surface of a smaller piece being fastened to a larger one is completely covered with glue.

Press fuselage flat between clean sheets of paper underneath a heavy weight (a few big books) until glue is sufficiently set (about 45 minutes).

**6** Glue 11B to the bottom of wing part 10W.

**7** Applying glue to the tail tabs, fasten horizontal stabilizer 12S to the fuselage.

**9** Camber the wings by curving the paper gently between thumb and forefinger. See below.

NOTE: Make sure wing parts are aligned along the centerline.

The dihedral angle of the wings must be set before the glue dries. See below.

**8** Applying glue to the wing tabs, fasten wing assembly to the fuselage.

Camber:

point of maximum camber, 30% from front

correct

too much

Dihedral: ¹/₂ in (1.25 cm)

NOTE: After completing the glider, it is important to let the glue set completely (an hour or two) before flying.

# Primary Glider

## Parts ✂

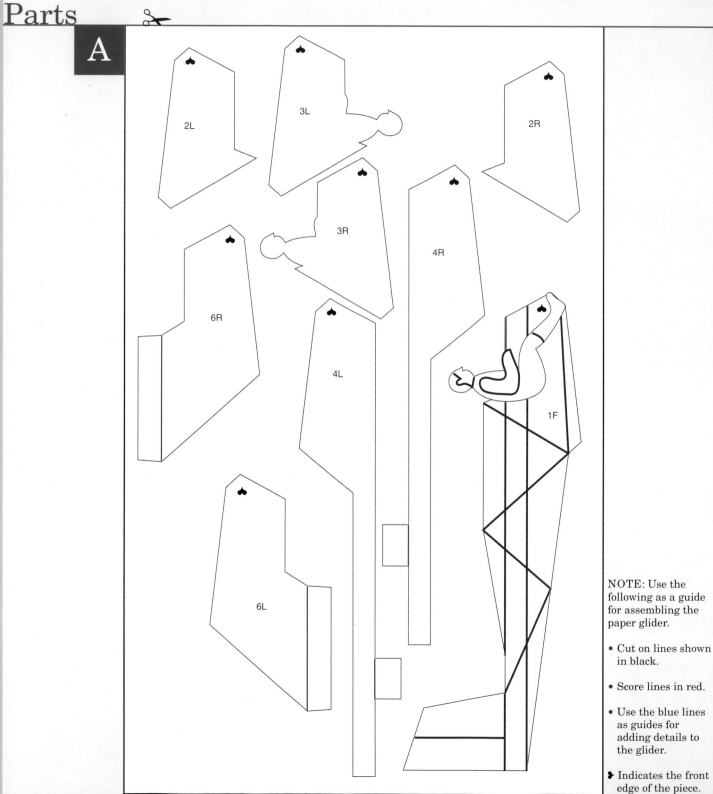

A

2L

3L

2R

3R

4R

6R

4L

1F

6L

NOTE: Use the following as a guide for assembling the paper glider.

- Cut on lines shown in black.

- Score lines in red.

- Use the blue lines as guides for adding details to the glider.

✦ Indicates the front edge of the piece.

First, photocopy these two pages (100% size). **Do not cut the pages from the book .**

Then cut out the portion indicated below from the photocopy.
This makes a cutting guide for the various parts and fits a
standard 5 x 8 inch index card. See page 33 for step two.

# Parts

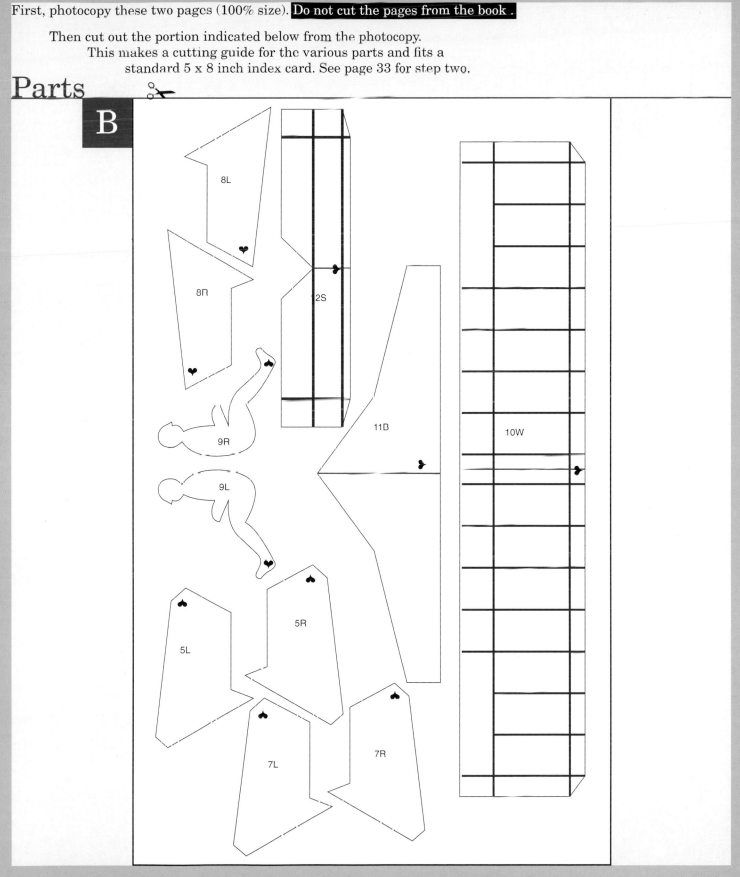

B

8L

8Π

2S

9R

9L

11B

10W

5R

5L

7L

7R

## Figure 11
Soaring flight in thermal lift

On a sunny day the earth is warmed by the sun's rays. This heat is radiated into the air which then becomes warmed. The warm air, being lighter, begins to form a bubble. It eventually breaks free, rises, and joins other bubbles becoming a column called a thermal. A glider circling inside this column can remain airborne as long as the air is rising as fast as or faster than the glider's sink rate. It can climb to the very top of the thermal, which is sometimes 10,000 feet (3000 m) or more in height. At the top of a thermal a cumulus cloud is often formed because the moist warm air from the ground rises into cold air aloft and the moisture condenses into a cloud. These clouds are important clues for glider pilots about where to find the next source of lift.

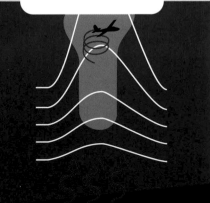

**W**HEN the first American national meet was held in 1930 meterological conditions necessary for soaring were just beginning to be understood by glider pilots. Largely unknown to American pilots was the fact that sustained flight was possible not only in ridge lift, but also over flatland warmed by the sun, in *thermal lift*. American pilots had sometimes encountered such lift away from the ridges, but flew right through it, not realizing that this lift ran in a vertical direction. The Germans, on the other hand, already knew how to use thermal lift but kept it a secret to maintain a competitive edge. German pilot Wolf Hirth used thermals to fly away from the ridges for a distance of 33 miles. His was the best flight of the meet. He was one of the top soaring pilots in the world at the time. Some time later he admitted that he had a "secret" instrument whereby areas of rising air could be determined. See figure 11.

Soon all glider pilots were no longer interested only in duration, but also in distances covered, speed, and altitudes gained. As the glide performance and flight characteristics of sailplanes improved, pilots became bolder in flying from one source of lift to another. Now thermal lift, which can be found anywhere, has surpassed ridge lift as the primary means of staying aloft in a sailplane because it gives the pilot freedom. And Hirth's "secret" instrument, the variometer, a sensitive rate-of-climb indicator, has become the soaring pilot's most important instrument.

By 1932 the NGA had been replaced by the Soaring Society of America, reflecting the shift in emphasis from gliding flight to soaring flight.

The SSA continued to hold national meets, and at the fifth American national meet in 1934 the distance record was pushed to 158 miles, and for the first time it was set by an American pilot, flying an American designed and built sailplane. But a month later at the 15th Wasserkuppe meet four German pilots exeeded the record, with Wolf Hirth in the lead having flown 218 miles. Altitudes in excess of 6000 feet, using thermal lift, were also attained. The Germans had developed the tight-turn spiraling technique of thermal soaring.

This technique was demonstrated to Americans for the first time at the 1937 American meet by German pilot, Peter Riedel. It has today become part of the standard training syllabus. That year also saw, for the first time, the aerotowing technique of launching used for competition sailplanes. It is now the standard launch method. In 1938 two-place training gliders were introduced to the U.S. For the first time it put the flight instructor into the cockpit with the student pilot, eliminating the need for instructions from the ground by hand signals and shouting.

World records kept climbing, and in 1938 the distance record was held by the Russians with 405 miles. An altitude of 14,189 feet had been attained by the Germans. American pilots realized the importance of location to record setting and used sites over the deserts where thermals were strong to achieve heights in excess of 10,000 feet (3000 m).

As in many parts of the world, Canadian soaring did not really get going until after the second world war. Before that time it was a disorganized effort: at best with local clubs setting their own standards and rules, at worst with individual "daredevils" building primary gliders in their backyards. But in 1939 Evelyn Fletcher, of the Lethbridge Gliding Club, flew a German Hütter II-17, for a distance of 10 miles, attaining an altitude of 4000 feet in a flight lasting 51 minutes, setting a Canadian record that was to stand for 10 years. In

the meantime, in 1944, the Soaring Association of Canada was formed to promote and organize motorless flight across the country.

By the end of the 1930s plans had been laid to make gliding an Olympic Event. This would have been a tremendous boost to the sport. But it was not to be. In the fall of 1939 Germany invaded Poland engulfing the world in war, and suspending the Games. Several designs had already been submitted as possible Olympic Sailplanes. One was the Orlik designed by H. Kocjan of Poland. **(Paper glider 5, p 38.)**

In 1938 the ninth American national soaring meet was won by Emil Lehecka flying a high performance German-built Rhoensperber glider.

text continues on page 56 . .

# Orlik

**5**

This glider was designed in Poland in the late 1930s for competition in the Olympic Games. It had an all-wood structure with fabric covering. Due to the war, the Olympic Games of 1940 were not held. In 1948, when the Games resumed, gliding was not among the events scheduled. However, the plane was used for other competitions. **(See text p 37.)**

# Instructions

NOTE: Also refer to general instructions on pp 6-9.

**1** See pages 40 and 41 for this step.

**2** Tack-glue parts cutting guides onto index cards by gluing on the **back-side between the parts**.

**3** Score the fold lines for wing and tail tabs. (After cutting out the pieces, bend tabs outward.)

**4** Cut each piece from the index card stock. Remove light-weight guide paper and discard, leaving a clean unmarked glider part.

NOTE: Cut carefully through both sheets. The cutting side is always the upward or outward facing surface of the finished part.

**5** Glue pieces 1F through 8R and 8L to build up fuselage layers, carefully aligning parts.

NOTE: Ensure that the entire contacting surface of a smaller piece being fastened to a larger one is completely covered with glue.

Press fuselage flat between clean sheets of paper underneath a heavy weight (a few big books) until glue is sufficiently set (about 45 minutes).

**6** Bring wing parts 9R and 9L together, fastening with 10T. Then glue 11R and 11L to the bottom of the wing. Finally glue 12B to the very bottom.

NOTE: Make sure wing parts are aligned along the centerline.

The dihedral angle of the wings must be set before the glue dries. See below.

**7** Applying glue to the tail tabs, fasten horizontal stabilizer 13S to the fuselage.

**8** Applying glue to the wing tabs, fasten wing assembly to the fuselage.

**9** Camber the wings by curving the paper gently between thumb and forefinger. See below.

10T

9L

11L

9R

11R

12B

13S

Camber:

point of maximum camber, 30% from front

correct

too much

Dihedral: 1 $\frac{1}{2}$ in (3.75 cm)

NOTE: After completing the glider, it is important to let the glue set completely (an hour or two) before flying.

1F 2L 3L 4L 5L 6L 7L 8L
2R 3R 4R 5R 6R 7R 8R

# Orlik

## Parts

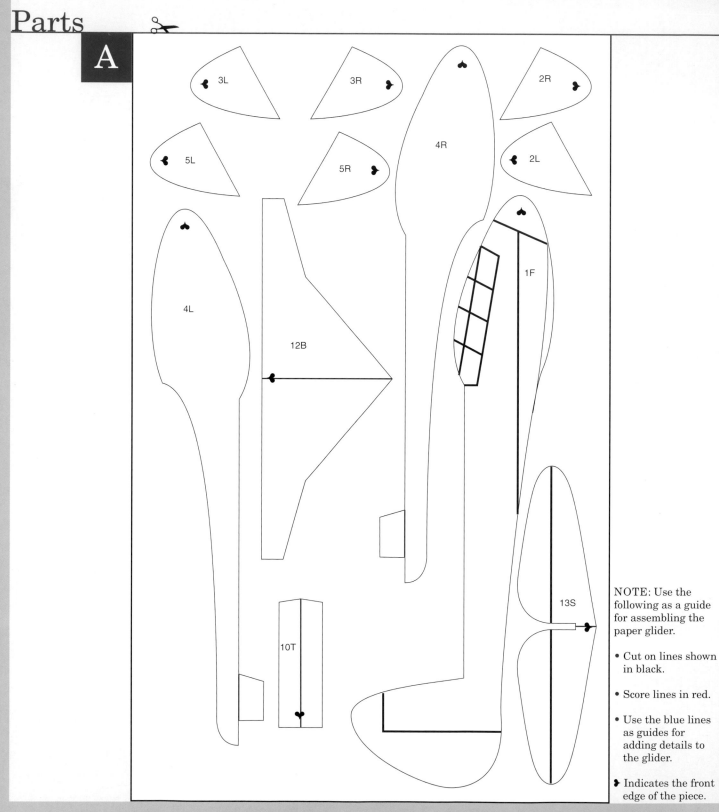

A

NOTE: Use the following as a guide for assembling the paper glider.

- Cut on lines shown in black.
- Score lines in red.
- Use the blue lines as guides for adding details to the glider.
- Indicates the front edge of the piece.

First, photocopy these two pages (100% size). <mark>Do not cut the pages from the book .</mark>

Then cut out the portion indicated below from the photocopy.
This makes a cutting guide for the various parts and fits a
standard 5 x 8 inch index card. See page 39 for step two.

# Parts

B

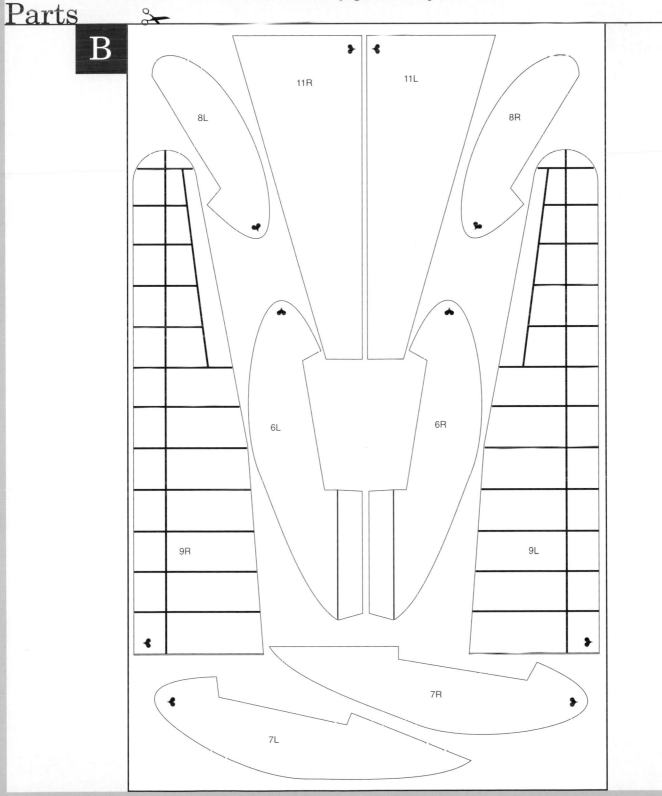

# Grunau Baby

**6**

The Grunau Baby, designed in Germany in 1928, is a simple all-wood framed and fabric covered glider of modest performance. It originally had a simple skid landing gear (no wheel). This little glider became very popular in Europe and elsewhere, with many thousands being built around the world over a period of years. **(See text p 56.)**

NOTE: Also refer to general instructions on pp 6-9.

**1** See pages 44 and 45 for this step.

**2** Tack-glue parts cutting guides onto index cards by gluing on the **back-side between the parts.**

**3** Score the fold lines for wing and tail tabs. (After cutting out the pieces, bend tabs outward.)

**4** Cut each piece from the index card stock. Remove light-weight guide paper and discard, leaving a clean unmarked glider part.

NOTE: Cut carefully through both sheets. The cutting side is always the upward or outward facing surface of the finished part.

7L
6L
5L
4L
3L
2L
1F
2R
3R
4R
5R
6R
7R

**5** Glue pieces 1F through 7R and 7L to build up fuselage layers, carefully aligning parts.

NOTE: Ensure that the entire contacting surface of a smaller piece being fastened to a larger one is completely covered with glue.

Press fuselage flat between clean sheets of paper underneath a heavy weight (a few big books) until glue is sufficiently set (about 45 minutes).

**6** Glue 9M to the bottom of wing part 8W. Then glue 10B to the bottom of 9M.

8W

9M

10B

**7** Applying glue to the tail tabs, fasten horizontal stabilizer 11S to the fuselage.

11S

**9** Camber the wings by curving the paper gently between thumb and forefinger. See below.

NOTE: Make sure wing parts are aligned along the centerline.

The dihedral angle of the wings must be set before the glue dries. See below.

**8** Applying glue to the wing tabs, fasten wing assembly to the fuselage.

Camber:

point of maximum camber, 30% from front

correct

too much

Dihedral: $^3/_4$ in (2 cm)

NOTE. After completing the glider, it is important to let the glue set completely (an hour or two) before flying.

# Grunau Baby

## Parts

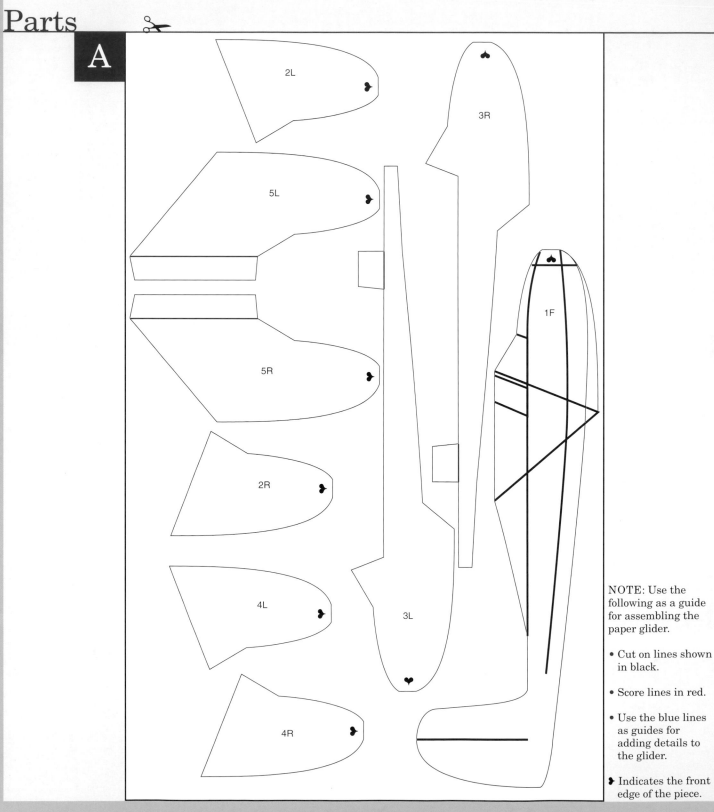

NOTE: Use the following as a guide for assembling the paper glider.

- Cut on lines shown in black.

- Score lines in red.

- Use the blue lines as guides for adding details to the glider.

➤ Indicates the front edge of the piece.

First, photocopy these two pages (100% size). <mark>Do not cut the pages from the book .</mark>

Then cut out the portion indicated below from the photocopy.
This makes a cutting guide for the various parts and fits a
standard 5 x 8 inch index card. See page 43 for step two.

# Parts

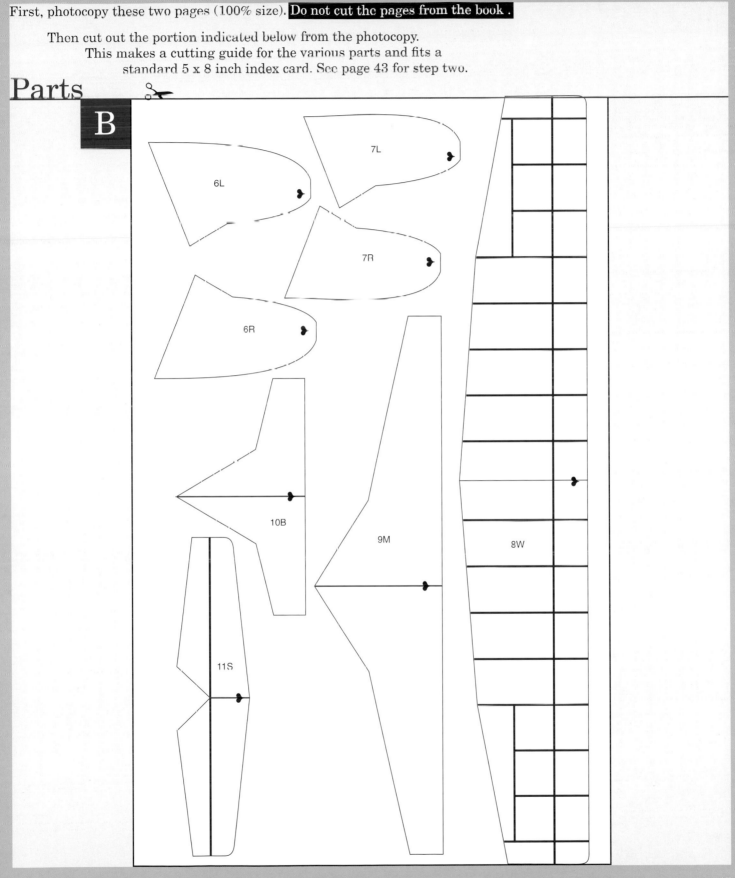

# Waco CG-4

This glider was designed by the Waco Aircraft Company and built by various manufacturers across the U.S. in large numbers as a military transport plane. It could carry any combination of either 15 fully equiped troops, a small field gun, a jeep, or a loaded trailer. The gliders were towed, usually in pairs, behind a powered transport aircraft such as the C-47 Dakota (which in civilian service was the Douglas DC-3). Once released they were a stealthy aircraft that could deliver troops and equipment behind enemy lines. The entire nose section, including the cockpit, tilted up, allowing for cargo access. **(See text p 56.)**

# Instructions

NOTE: Also refer to general instructions on pp 6-9.

**1** See pages 54 and 55 for this step.

**2** Tack-glue parts cutting guides onto index cards by gluing on the **backside between the parts**.

**4** Cut each piece from the index card stock. Remove lightweight guide paper and discard, leaving a clean unmarked glider part.

NOTE: Cut carefully through both sheets. The cutting side is always the upward or outward facing surface of the finished part.

**3** Score the fold lines for wing and tail tabs. (After cutting out the pieces, bend tabs outward.)

**5** Glue pieces 1F through 8R and 8L to build up fuselage layers, carefully aligning parts.

NOTE: Ensure that the entire contacting surface of a smaller piece being fastened to a larger one is completely covered with glue.

Press fuselage flat between clean sheets of paper underneath a heavy weight (a few big books) until glue is sufficiently set (about 45 minutes).

**6** Glue 10B to the bottom of wing part 9W.

9W

10B

NOTE: Make sure wing parts are aligned along the centerline.

The dihedral angle of the wings must be set before the glue dries. See below.

**7** Applying glue to the tail tabs, fasten horizontal stabilizer 11S to the fuselage.

11S

**9** Camber the wings by curving the paper gently between thumb and forefinger. See below.

**8** Applying glue to the wing tabs, fasten wing assembly to the fuselage.

Camber:

point of maximum camber, 30% from front

correct

too much

Dihedral: 3/4 in (2 cm)

NOTE: After completing the glider, it is important to let the glue set completely (an hour or two) before flying.

# Colditz Cock

## Parts

**A**

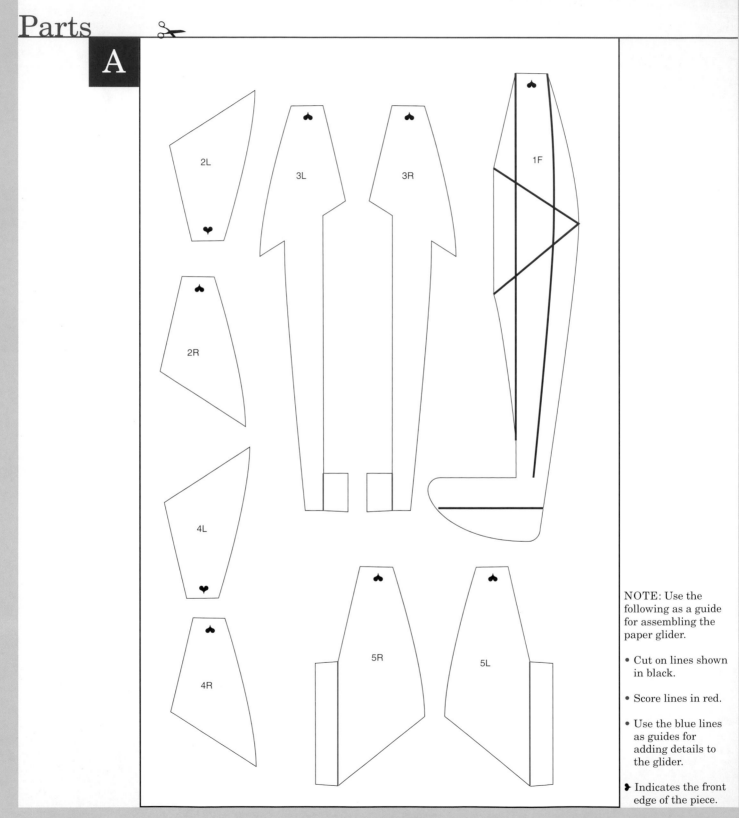

NOTE: Use the following as a guide for assembling the paper glider.

- Cut on lines shown in black.

- Score lines in red.

- Use the blue lines as guides for adding details to the glider.

➤ Indicates the front edge of the piece.

First, photocopy these two pages (100% size). 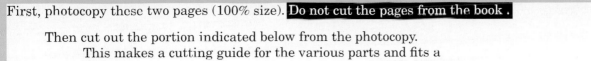 Do not cut the pages from the book .

Then cut out the portion indicated below from the photocopy.
This makes a cutting guide for the various parts and fits a
standard 5 x 8 inch index card. See page 53 for step two.

# Parts

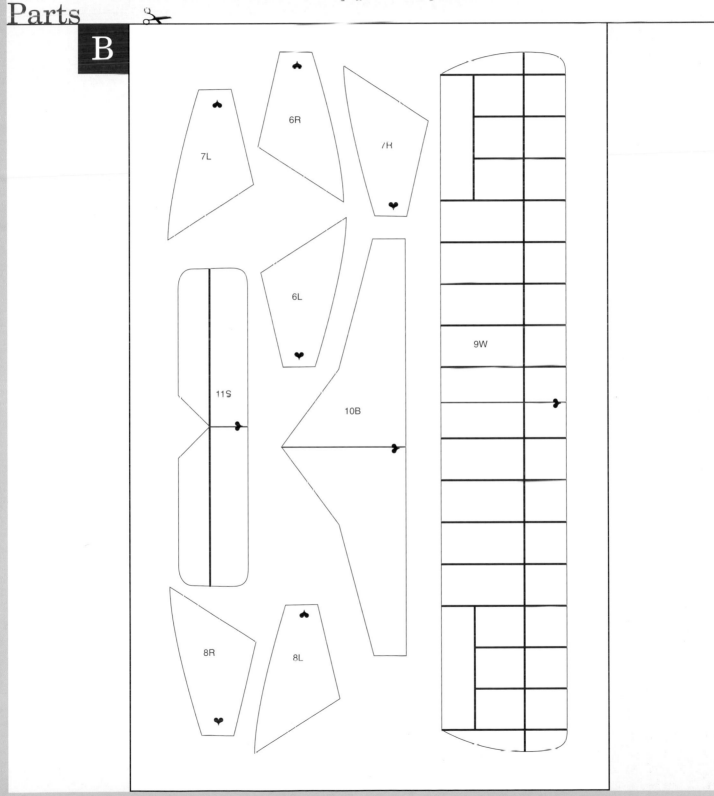

B

7L

6R

7R

6L

11S

10B

9W

8R

8L

**URING** the second world war Germany was first to make use of gliders for pilot training and the transport of troops and equipment. The Grunau Baby of the 1930s was a single seat glider in widespread use. More than 6000 of them were built. Many of the German Luftwaffe pilots had flown this glider prior to becoming fighter pilots. This was an important aircraft. Its popularity was instrumental in generating interest in gliding, not only in Germany, but across Europe. **(Paper glider 6, p 42.)**

In 1941 the U.S. government followed Germany's lead and undertook a nationwide glider training program. The Schweizer Aircraft Corporation was established at Elmira, New York to build gliders, and the first two-place instructional glider they made was selected as a military trainer, the TG-2.

Both sides in the conflict built combat gliders. The Allies had the British Horsa and the American Waco CG-4 for troop and equipment transport. Both were built in large numbers (14,000 CG-4s were built) and used for tactical battle maneuvers. The Axis had similar machines. All gliders were towed either singley or in pairs behind powered transport planes carrying paratroopers, and were used mainly for night invasion. Each of the gliders could carry about 5000 pounds (2250 kg) of equipment or troops. Once released from the tow plane, they could silently penetrate behind enemy lines.

The Horsa and the CG-4 played an important role in the liberation of Europe, with more than 500 gliders being flown in the initial invasion of Normandy in 1944. They were also used in other theaters of war, most notably in Burma, where 54 CG-4s took a force of engineers 100 miles behind enemy lines to establish a landing stronghold deep in the jungle. After one week they had successfully brought in 9,000 fully equipped troops. **(Paper glider 7, p 46.)**

During the war Colditz Castle, situated on the cliffs of Saxony, became a Prisoner of War camp. Bill Goldfinch, a British Flying Officer POW, designed a small glider which was built by fellow prisoners from materials in the camp and was to be used to escape the castle. Floorboards became wing spars, the ribs and frame were made from bed slats, and control lines were electrical wiring, all surreptitiously obtained. The covering was cotton which came from sleeping bags, sealed with a slurry made by boiling down prison ration millet. The war ended before the glider could be used but later a model was built and flown. **(Paper glider 8, p 52.)**

## Figure 12

Soaring flight in wave lift

When air is forced upward over high mountains it behaves much like water that flows around stones in a river. Both form ripples and waves. These waves in air over mountains are often accompanied by lozenge-shaped clouds. A glider flown into wave lift can climb to extremely high altitudes — the very limits at which a human can live without a pressure suit. A supply of oxygen must be carried on board.

**A**FTER the war ended in 1945 aviators once again could turn to sport flying, and by the mid 1950s gliding and soaring had spread to most developed countries. The sport became well organized and the period was marked by research in material use, aerodynamics, meteorology, and soaring techniques.

As early as the mid-1930s German pilots had been aware of lift to very high altitudes near lozenge-shaped clouds over mountains. These clouds form as air is forced upward over mountain peaks and forms waves, much as ripples are formed around stones in a river. This source of lift is called *wave lift*. Before the days of aerotow launching it was difficult to reach. In 1947 Paul MacCready, flying an Orlik, climbed to an altitude of 21,000 feet (6300 m) over the Sierra Nevada mountains, beginning a trend at setting high altitude records. See figure 12.

The International Scientific and Technical Organization (OSTIV) made a standard body of research widely available, resulting in an increasing number of factory-built gliders for training and soaring.

Before the war German glider designers had experimented with lightweight alloy metal structures, slender fuselages with narrow eliptical cross-sections, small canopies, cantilevered (no bracing) high aspect ratio wings, and larger rudders. (For example, the Cirrus D-30, with a wingspan of 65 feet (20 m) and an aspect ratio of 33, whose performance was not surpassed until 1954.)

New world-wide research into materials and methods resulted in a widespread change in how gliders were built after the war. Great improvement could be achieved by using different airfoil cross-sectional shapes (see figure 13), and by reducing waviness in wings, using unbroken polished surfaces, adding rounded fairings, and removing even small gaps and air leaks.

The aspect ratio of wings and wing strength was constantly researched (see figure 14). World-wide research and sharing of knowledge led to the universal classification of sailplanes by performance levels. Standard Class defined the average sailplane. Mass produced sailplanes continually improved in quality and performance. Manufacturers used a variety of materials in sailplanes, often in one machine —wood, steel, aluminum, fabric, and fiberglass.

Immediately after the war most American glider manufacturers went out of business. Only the Schweizer Aircraft Corporation remained. Besides two-place training gliders, Schweizer also introduced high-performance single-seat sailplanes. Most glider pilots in North America since the mid 1950s have received their pilot training in a Schweizer glider.

War planes had been made mainly of metal — steel and alloy frames with lightweight riveted aluminum skins, yeilding good performance. This is the technology utilized by the Schweizers in glider construction. It proved to be ideal — the right weight for sailplanes, its strength afforded good pilot protection in the event of a crash, its smoothness gave the desired finish for reducing drag, and it was dura-

## Figure 13

Airfoil cross-sections

Lilienthal used only a single skin over a curved frame, like an umbrella, to make wings for his gliders. Since the first world war there has been a steady evolution in the the cross-section shape of glider wings in the interest of creating higher lift to drag ratios and good performance. The thicker the wing, the greater the pressure drag. Also, the more difficult it is for air to flow smoothly around the curve. Different shapes operate at their own best angle of attack and airspeed. Therefore different thicknesses, positions of the point of maximum camber, shape of the lower surface, and positions of the trailing edge have been tried. Since the second world war wings have been made over which airflow closely follows the contour of the upper surface (laminar flow) for improved performance over a wider speed range. Some wings (not shown) have camber changing flaps at the trailing edge to decrease lift at higher speeds and increase it at lower speeds, giving the glider an even wider optimum speed range.

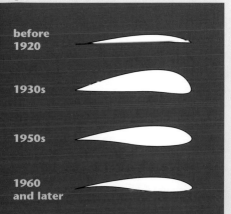

before 1920

1930s

1950s

1960 and later

## Figure 14

The aspect ratio of sailplane wings

Research has proven that the longer a wing is in relation to the distance from its leading to trailing edge (higher aspect ratio) the greater its efficiency, having lower induced drag. Since the days of Lilienthal there has, therefore, been a steady increase in the aspect ratio of glider wings in the interest of improving glide ratios. The highest today is over 30:1. Most, however, are around 20. Correspondingly, wingspans, too, have increased. Most are between 48 and 54 feet (15-17 m). Greater spans make handling on the ground and in the air more difficult.

There is also a relationship between aspect ratio and a wing's thickness, as there is only so much strength that can be built into a wing of a given thickness. Early gliders all had struts to support the wings. Since the second world war, with the use of stronger materials, wings have been internally supported (cantilevered). In wings of high aspect ratio torsional strength, to keep them from distorting under load, requires careful and critical engineering.

High aspect ratio wings is one feature that distinguishes gliders from other aircraft.

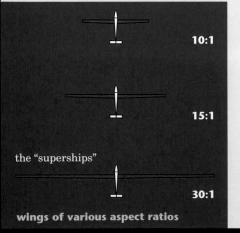

10:1

15:1

the "superships"

30:1

**wings of various aspect ratios**

ble. The Schweizers produced just the kind of gliders that would be attractive to the growing club market.

One Schweizer single-seat glider was the SGS 1-26. It had a steel tube frame with an alloy wing structure, aluminum and fabric skin, and a fiberglass nose. To keep costs down, it was originally planned as a kit, simple enough for the average person to assemble in the home garage without special tools. But soon it was produced also as a factory-built model. In total 700 of them were produced between 1954 and 1979.

It has become one of the most popular sailplanes in North America. Like the Grunau Baby in Europe, it was instrumental in popularizing the sport of soaring. Although it has been superseded in performance, and no longer ranks among the high-performance ships, most of the 1-26s built remain in active service as a favorite personal sport glider for many pilots, having become an "American Classic." It holds many records. The 1-26 Association was formed for pilots of this glider to exchange soaring ideas and to compete with one another. **(Paper glider 9, p 60.)**

Because aircraft designers were familiar with wood and fabric, and these materials were economical, gliders continued to be built from them. Skilled craftsmen were able to attain high performance using these materials. One example is the Sagitta, the first Standard Class sailplane produced in Holland. Another is the Schleicher Ka-6. It has become world famous for its good performance, winning the 1958 OSTIV award

for the best Standard Class sailplane, as well as setting many flight records. **(Paper glider 10, p 64.)**

Some fine all-metal two-place gliders were built in Eastern Europe. One is the Blanik L-13, produced by the Czech Aeronautical Research Center. It is of steel and aluminum contruction with fabric covered control surfaces. Beginning in 1956 more than 2000 were produced. Outside of North America it remains the most common trainer and can be used for aerobatics. Another is the Lark from Romania. Because of its high performance, it has become popular world wide. It is also available as a single-seat model. **(Paper glider 11, p 68.)**

Among the innovations of the postwar period were flying wing sailplanes. In 1937 German engineer, Dr. Reimar Horton, built the first flying wing aircraft — aircraft without fuselages and whose wings provide both lift and stability. With some modifications, this configuration was utilized after the war by Witold Kasper, Jim Marske, and others. The Marske Pioneer, developed from a wood and fabric covered design of 1957, is popular in North America.

Mixed material construction yielded good sailplanes in all classes, but in 1964 the molded all-fiberglass Libelle was introduced by the German Glasflügel company, setting a new standard in smoothness.

**B**Y the 1970s soaring had come of age, no longer limited to a few participants. The sport had grown sufficiently around the world that there were enough pilots of exceptional skill to warrant regular international competition, and many countries sent teams of their best to compete in the World Soaring Championships. In 1970 they were held in the United States for the first time and astronaut Niel Armstrong, who the year before had been first to land on the moon, was the official presidential representative at the event. He was the pilot of a Libelle 201 and a Schweizer 1-26.

It became apparent that the added performance of fiberglass ships was advantageous to pilots competing at national and international levels, and the composite construction techniques introduced by Glasflügel were copied by other manufacturers. The Standard Class became primarily a class of "glass slippers" — sleek fiberglass ships. Those manufacturers who did not adopt fiberglass went out of business or turned to other things — Schweizer no longer produces gliders.

In composite construction the frame is eliminated. Thin layers of strong fibers are molded into the glider's shape, infused with resin, and cured. This skin is strong, seamless, and smooth. With this technique Standard Class glide ratios increased from about 30:1 to nearly 40:1.

People have always enjoyed aerial displays. This prompted Ursula Hänle, whose husband designed the Libelle, to build a glider for just this purpose in 1971, the all-fiberglass Salto H-101. **(Paper glider 12, p 72.)**

Gliders with motors, for use when no source of lift can be found, were introduced. One example is the 1982 canard wing Solitaire, by Burt Rutan. The motor and propeller pop up out of its long nose when needed. **(Paper glider 13, p 76.)**

Composite construction is also compatible with computer aided design techniques, which allow for very precise aerodynamic measurements to be made. Jim Marske used this method for developing a new ultra-efficient glider, the Genesis, which was first flown in 1993. It is a hybrid design combining concepts from flying wing and regular aircraft. **(Paper glider 14, p 80.)**

By the mid 1980s the cost of Standard Class sailplanes had risen beyond the average person's reach, causing for the call of a new economical design. It was to be not only affordable but also a contender for Olympic competition. (Soaring is scheduled as an Olympic event in the year 2000.) A design competition was held. The winning design was the Polish PW-5 Smyk, certified in 1994. **(Paper glider 15, p 84.)**

Because soaring is a competitive sport, performance improvements at any cost continue to be made. Composite technology allows for the use of exotic materials such as kevlar and carbon fibers, having extraordinary strength for their weight, and allowing for the construction of ultra-high aspect ratio "superships" — gliders of exceptional performance. Examples are the Schleicher AS-W 22 and Schemp-Hirth Nimbus 4, the world's two highest performers, having glide ratios of over 60:1. **(Paper glider 16, p 88.)**

text continues on page 93

# Schweizer SGS 1-26

9

The Schweizer SGS 1-26, first introduced as an economical glider to promote one-class competition in the early fifties, has become a favorite personal sport glider used for weekend recreational soaring as well as to set many records. Early models were metal framed with fabric covering, later ones were all metal. **(See text p 58.)**

# Instructions

NOTE: Also refer to general instructions on pp 6-9.

**1** See pages 62 and 63 for this step.

**2** Tack-glue parts cutting guides onto index cards by gluing on the **back-side between the parts**.

**3** Cut opening for wings in fuselage part.

**4** Score the fold lines for wing and tail tabs. (After cutting out the pieces, bend tabs outward.)

**5** Cut each piece from the index card stock. Remove light-weight guide paper and discard, leaving a clean unmarked glider part.

**6** Glue pieces 1F through 7R and 7L to build up fuselage layers, carefully aligning parts.

NOTE: Cut carefully through both sheets. The cutting side is always the upward or outward facing surface of the finished part.

NOTE: Ensure that the entire contacting surface of a smaller piece being fastened to a larger one is completely covered with glue.

**7** Bring wing parts 8R and 8L together, fastening with 9T. Then glue 10M to the bottom of the wing. Finally glue 11B to the very bottom.

Press fuselage flat between clean sheets of paper underneath a heavy weight (a few big books) until glue is sufficiently set (about 45 minutes).

**8** Applying glue to the tail tabs, fasten horizontal stabilizer 12S to the fuselage.

**10** Camber the wings by curving the paper gently between thumb and forefinger. See below

NOTE: Make sure wing parts are aligned along the centerline.

The dihedral angle of the wings must be set before the glue dries. See below.

**9** Applying glue to the wing tabs, fasten wing assembly to the fuselage.

Camber:

point of maximum camber, 30% from front

correct

too much

Dihedral: 1 in (2.5 cm)

NOTE: After completing the glider, it is important to let the glue set completely (an hour or two) before flying.

# Schweizer SGS 1-26

## Parts

A

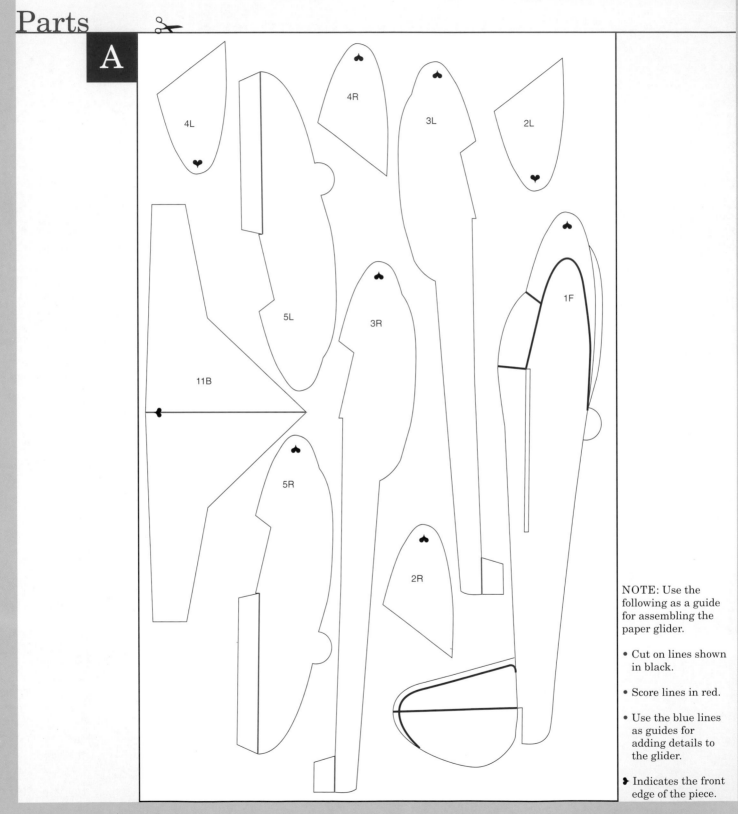

NOTE: Use the following as a guide for assembling the paper glider.

- Cut on lines shown in black.

- Score lines in red.

- Use the blue lines as guides for adding details to the glider.

➤ Indicates the front edge of the piece.

First, photocopy these two pages (100% size). **Do not cut the pages from the book .**

Then cut out the portion indicated below from the photocopy.
This makes a cutting guide for the various parts and fits a
standard 5 x 8 inch index card. See page 61 for step two.

# Parts

## B

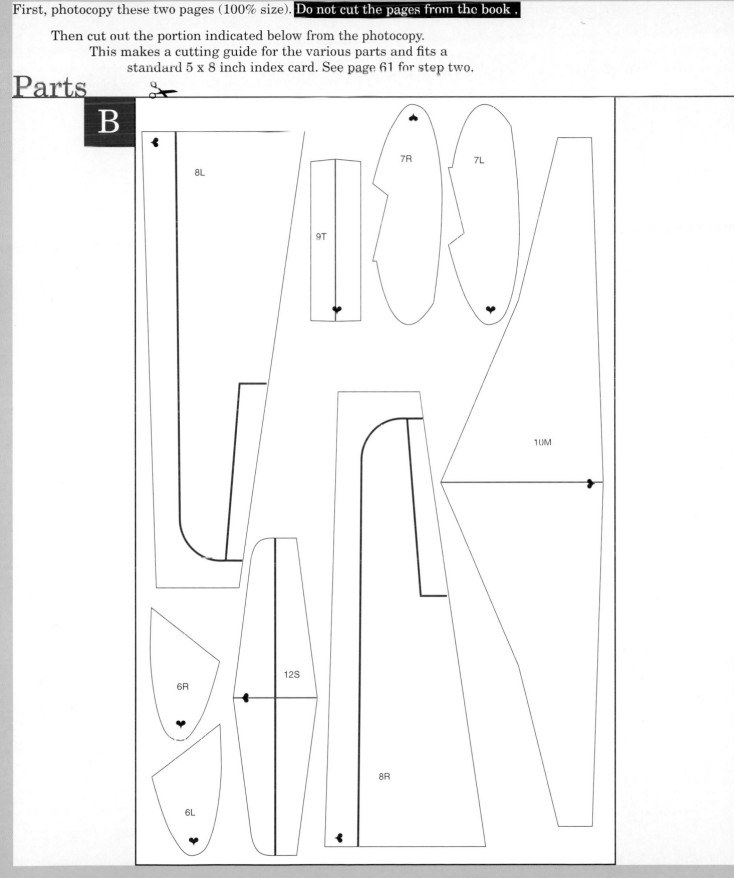

# Schleicher Ka-6

This is an all-wood aircraft, including most of the covering. It has become world famous for its many accomplishments, winning awards for both design and good flights. In 1963 two were flown from Germany to France for a world distance record that stood until 1969. More than 500 were built. **(See text p 58.)**

# Instructions

NOTE: Also refer to general instructions on pp 6-9.

**1** See pages 66 and 67 for this step.

**2** Tack-glue parts cutting guides onto index cards by gluing on the **back-side between the parts**.

**3** Cut opening in fuselage part for horizontal stabilizer.

**4** Score the fold lines for wing and tail tabs. (After cutting out the pieces, bend tabs outward.)

**5** Cut each piece from the index card stock. Remove light-weight guide paper and discard, leaving a clean unmarked glider part.

NOTE: Cut carefully through both sheets. The cutting side is always the upward or outward facing surface of the finished part.

**6** Glue pieces 1F through 4R and 4L to build up fuselage layers, carefully aligning parts.

4L
3L
2L
1F
2R
3R
4R

NOTE: Ensure that the entire contacting surface of a smaller piece being fastened to a larger one is completely covered with glue.

Press fuselage flat between clean sheets of paper underneath a heavy weight (a few big books) until glue is sufficiently set (about 45 minutes).

**7** Bring wing parts 5R and 5L together, fastening with 6T. Then glue 7R and 7L to the bottom of the wing. Finally glue 8B to the very bottom.

5L
6T
7L
5R
7R
8B

NOTE: Make sure wing parts are aligned along the centerline.

The dihedral angle of the wings must be set before the glue dries. See below.

**8** Applying glue to the tail tabs, fasten horizontal stabilizer 9S to the fuselage.

9S

**9** Applying glue to the wing tabs, fasten wing assembly to the fuselage.

**10** Camber the wings by curving the paper gently between thumb and forefinger. See below.

Camber:

point of maximum camber, 30% from front

correct

too much

Dihedral: 1 1/2 in (3.75 cm)

NOTE: After completing the glider, it is important to let the glue set completely (an hour or two) before flying.

# Schleicher Ka-6

## Parts

A

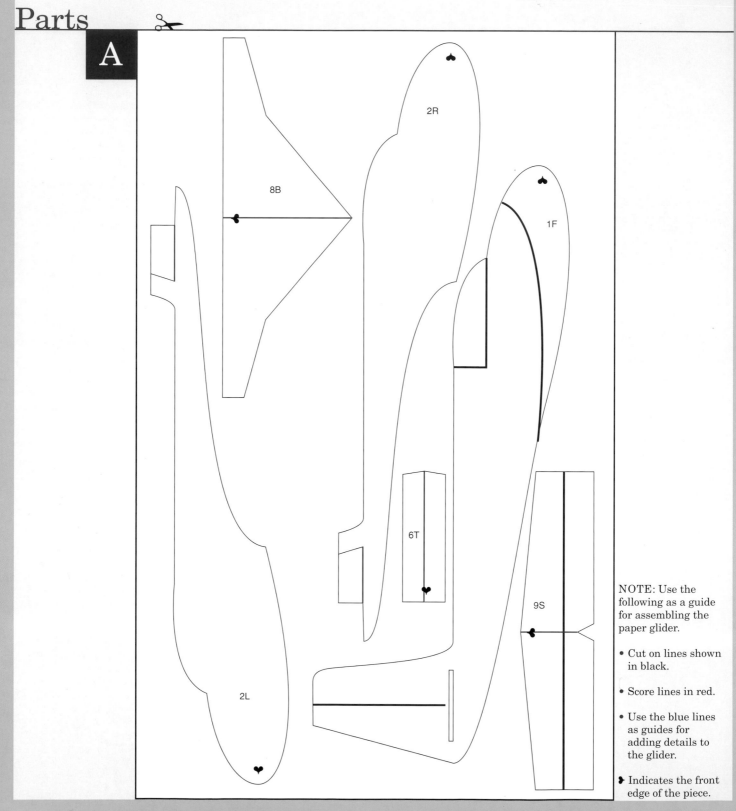

8B

2R

1F

6T

9S

2L

NOTE: Use the following as a guide for assembling the paper glider.

• Cut on lines shown in black.

• Score lines in red.

• Use the blue lines as guides for adding details to the glider.

❥ Indicates the front edge of the piece.

First, photocopy these two pages (100% size). **Do not cut the pages from the book .**

Then cut out the portion indicated below from the photocopy.
This makes a cutting guide for the various parts and fits a
standard 5 x 8 inch index card. See page 65 for step two.

# Parts

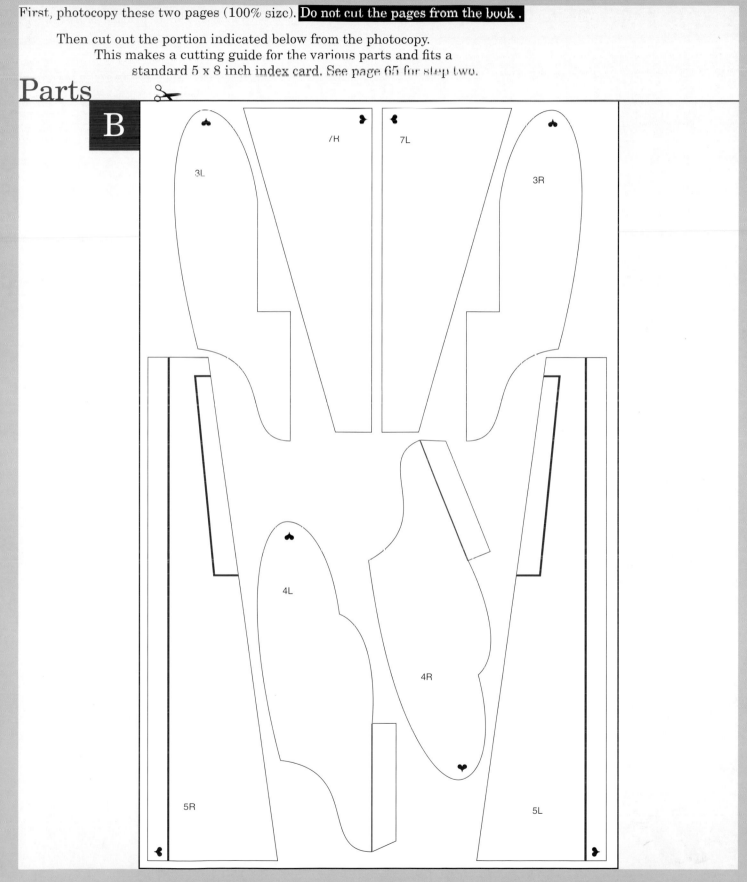

# Lark I.S. 28B2

## 11

This large two-place glider is of all-metal construction and has a gross weight of 1300 pounds (585 kg). Despite its large size, it has good performance with camber changing flaps on its wings. More than 300 of this glider have been produced. It is also available in a smaller single-seat model, the I.S.29D2. **(See text p 58.)**

# Instructions

**1** See pages 70 and 71 for this step.

**2** Tack-glue parts cutting guides onto index cards by gluing on the **back-side between the parts**.

**4** Cut each piece from the index card stock. Remove light-weight guide paper and discard, leaving a clean unmarked glider part.

NOTE: Cut carefully through both sheets. The cutting side is always the upward or outward facing surface of the finished part.

**3** Score the fold lines for wing and tail tabs. (After cutting out the pieces, bend tabs outward.)

5L
4L
3L
2L
1F
2R
3R
4R
5R

NOTE: Ensure that the entire contacting surface of a smaller piece being fastened to a larger one is completely covered with glue.

**5** Glue pieces 1F through 5R and 5L to build up fuselage layers, carefully aligning parts.

Press fuselage flat between clean sheets of paper underneath a heavy weight (a few big books) until glue is sufficiently set (about 45 minutes).

**6** Bring wing parts 6R and 6L together, fastening with 7T. Then add 8R + 8L and 9R + 9L to the bottom of the wing. Finally glue 10B to the very bottom.

6L
7T
8L
9L
6R
8R
9R
10B
11S

**7** Applying glue to the tail tabs, fasten horizontal stabilizer 11S to the fuselage.

**9** Camber the wings by curving the paper gently between thumb and forefinger. See below.

NOTE: Make sure wing parts are aligned along the centerline.

The dihedral angle of the wings must be set before the glue dries. See below.

**8** Applying glue to the wing tabs, fasten wing assembly to the fuselage.

Camber:

point of maximum camber, 30% from front

correct

too much

Dihedral: 1 1/2 in (3.75 cm)

NOTE: After completing the glider, it is important to let the glue set completely (an hour or two) before flying.

## Parts

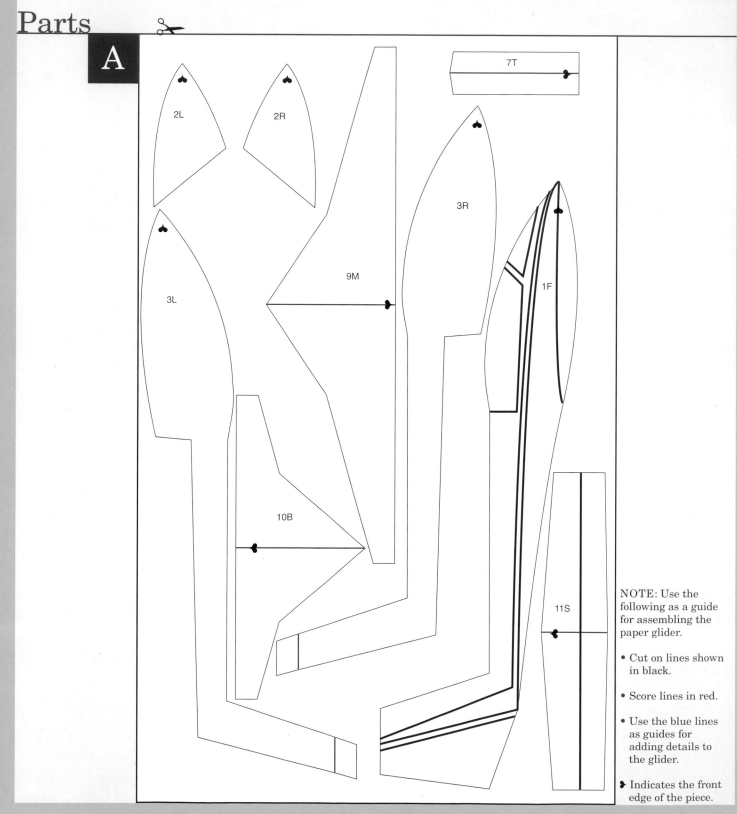

A

2L

2R

7T

3R

3L

9M

1F

10B

11S

NOTE: Use the following as a guide for assembling the paper glider.

• Cut on lines shown in black.

• Score lines in red.

• Use the blue lines as guides for adding details to the glider.

➤ Indicates the front edge of the piece.

First, photocopy these two pages (100% size). Do not cut the pages from the book .

Then cut out the portion indicated below from the photocopy.
This makes a cutting guide for the various parts and fits a
standard 5 x 8 inch index card. See page 69 for step two.

# Parts

## B

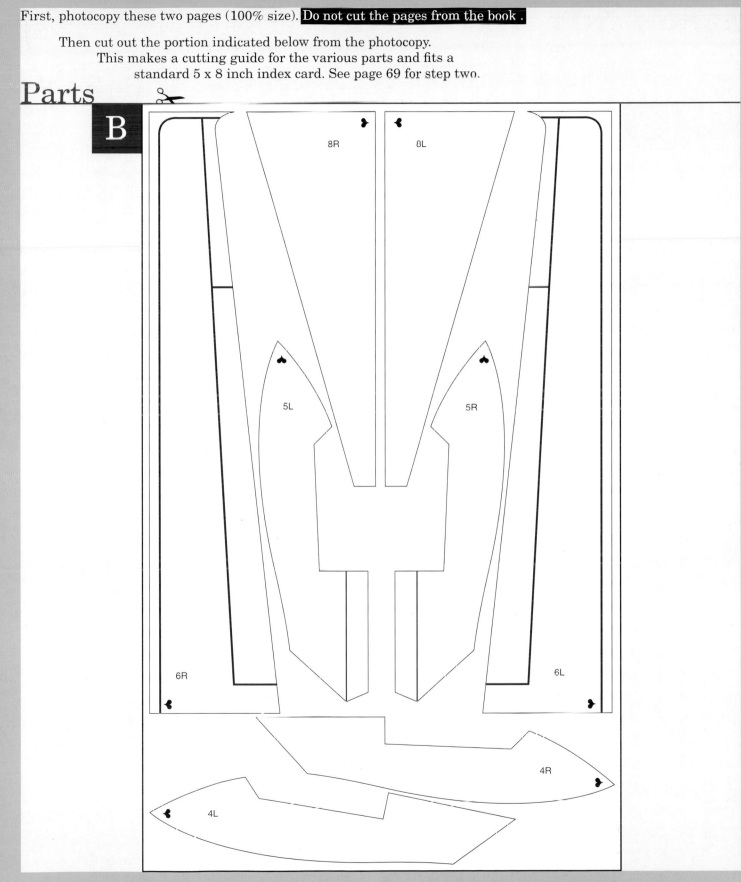

# Salto H-101

## 12

Salto means summersault in German. This all-fiberglass glider is designed to do aerobatic flying. Since the early days of aviation people have been thrilled by the sight of aerial displays consisting of rolls, loops, and spins. For maneuverability this glider has a relatively short wingspan and a large V-shaped tail. It uses some parts in common with the Libelle. **(See text p 59.)**

# Instructions

NOTE: Also refer to general instructions on pp 6-9.

**1** See pages 74 and 75 for this step.

**2** Tack-glue parts cutting guides onto index cards by gluing on the **back-side between the parts.**

**3** Cut opening for wings in fuselage part.

**5** Cut each piece from the index card stock. Remove light-weight guide paper and discard, leaving a clean unmarked glider part.

**4** Score the fold lines for wing and tail tabs. (After cutting out the pieces, bend tabs outward.)

NOTE: Cut carefully through both sheets. The cutting side is always the upward or outward facing surface of the finished part.

NOTE: Ensure that the entire contacting surface of a smaller piece being fastened to a larger one is completely covered with glue.

**6** Glue pieces 1F through 6R and 6L to build up fuselage layers, carefully aligning parts.

Press fuselage flat between clean sheets of paper underneath a heavy weight (a few big books) until glue is sufficiently set (about 45 minutes).

**7** Bring wing parts 7R and 7L together, fastening with 8T. Then glue 9R and 9L to the bottom of the wing. Finally glue 10B to the very bottom.

**8** Applying glue to the tail tabs and fasten V-tail 11V to the fuselage, adjusting dihedral to 45 degrees.

**10** Camber the wings by curving the paper gently between thumb and forefinger. See below.

NOTE: Make sure wing parts are aligned along the centerline.

The dihedral angle of the wings must be set before the glue dries. See below.

**9** Applying glue to the wing tabs, fasten wing assembly to the fuselage.

Camber:

point of maximum camber, 30% from front

correct

too much

Dihedral: 1 1/4 in (3 cm)

NOTE: After completing the glider, it is important to let the glue set completely (an hour or two) before flying.

Labels: 1F, 2R, 2L, 3R, 3L, 4R, 4L, 5R, 5L, 6R, 6L, 7L, 7R, 8T, 9L, 9R, 10B, 11V

# Salto H-101

## Parts

**A**

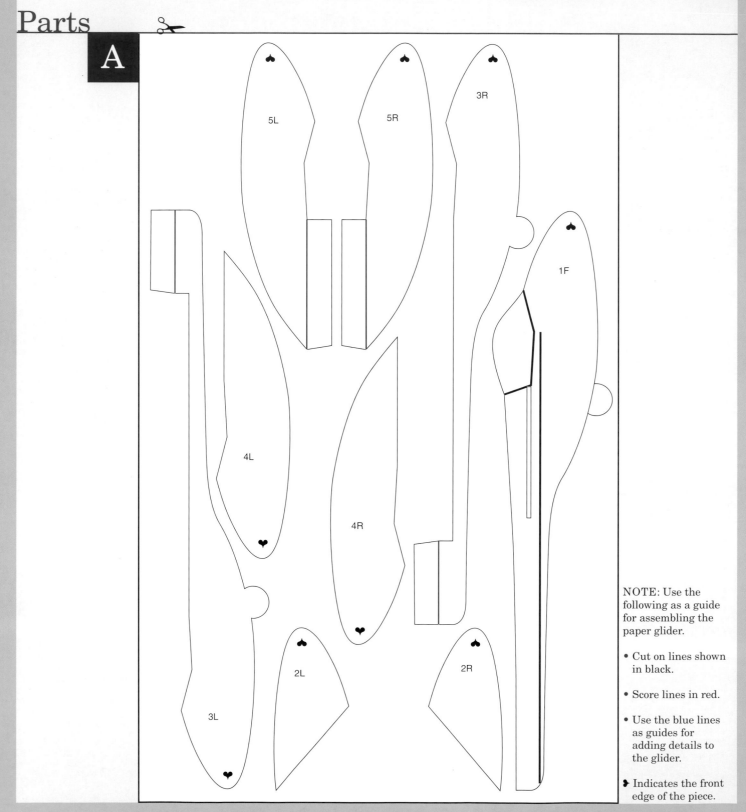

NOTE: Use the following as a guide for assembling the paper glider.

- Cut on lines shown in black.

- Score lines in red.

- Use the blue lines as guides for adding details to the glider.

➤ Indicates the front edge of the piece.

First, photocopy these two pages (100% size). Do not cut the pages from the book .

Then cut out the portion indicated below from the photocopy.
This makes a cutting guide for the various parts and fits a
standard 5 x 8 inch index card. See page 73 for step two.

# Parts

## B

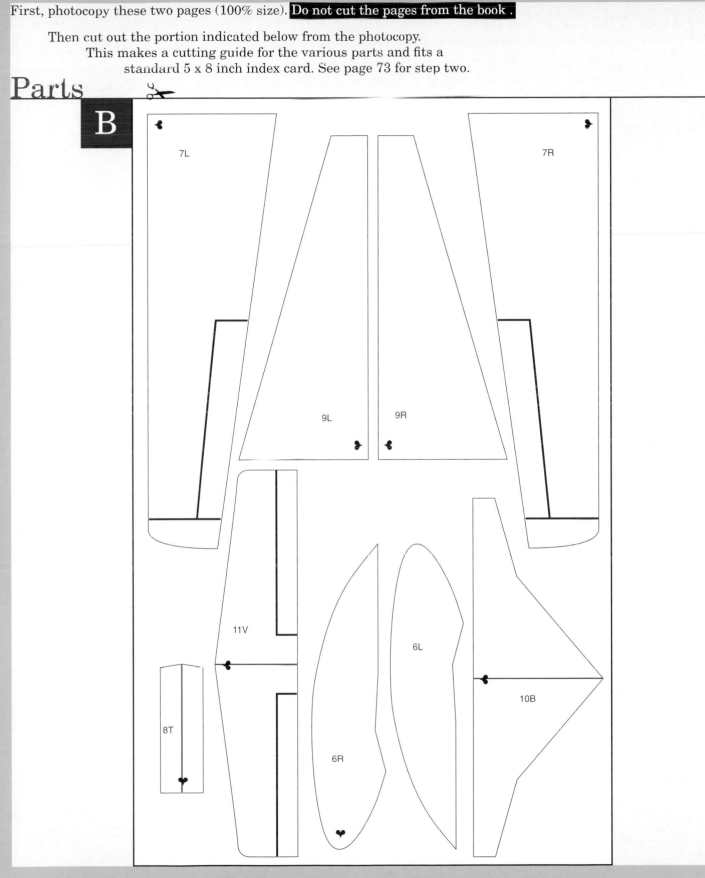

7L

7R

9L

9R

11V

6L

8T

10B

6R

# Solitaire Canard

13

Canards have small wings ahead of the main ones, necessitating a longer nose, which makes the planes look like long-necked ducks. (Canard means duck in French.) Aircraft designer, Burt Rutan, is known for his wide variety of canard aircraft. This glider is unusual not only because it is a canard, but also because it is a motorglider, which allows it to remain aloft even when no sources of lift are present. It is of all-fiberglass construction. **(See text p 59.)**

# Instructions

NOTE: Also refer to general instructions on pp 6-9.

**1** See pages 78 and 79 for this step.

**2** Tack-glue parts cutting guides onto index cards by gluing on the **back-side between the parts**.

**3** Cut opening for wings in fuselage parts.

**5** Cut each piece from the index card stock. Remove light-weight guide paper and discard, leaving a clean unmarked glider part.

**4** Score the fold lines for wing and tail tabs. (After cutting out the pieces, bend tabs outward.)

NOTE: Cut carefully through both sheets. The cutting side is always the upward or outward facing surface of the finished part.

6L 5L 4L 3L 2L 1F 2R 1F 3R 2R 4R 5R 6R

NOTE: Ensure that the entire contacting surface of a smaller piece being fastened to a larger one is completely covered with glue.

**6** Glue pieces 1F through 6R and 6L to build up fuselage layers, carefully aligning parts.

**7** Glue 12B to the bottom of the canard wing piece 11C.

11C
12B

Press fuselage flat between clean sheets of paper underneath a heavy weight (a few big books) until glue is sufficiently set (about 45 minutes).

**8** Bring wing parts 7R and 7L together, fastening with 8T. Then glue 9R and 9L to the bottom of the wing. Finally glue 10B to the very bottom.

7L
8T
9L
7R 9R 10B

**9** Applying glue to the wing tabs, fasten main wing assembly to the fuselage.

**11** Camber the wings by curving the paper gently between thumb and forefinger. See below.

NOTE: Make sure wing parts are aligned along the centerline.

The dihedral angle of the wings must be set before the glue dries. See below.

**10** Applying glue to the wing tabs, fasten canard wing assembly to the fuselage.

Camber:

point of maximum camber, 30% from front

correct

too much

Dihedral: 1 1/4 in (3 cm)

NOTE: After completing the glider, it is important to let the glue set completely (an hour or two) before flying.

# Solitaire Canard

## Parts

**A**

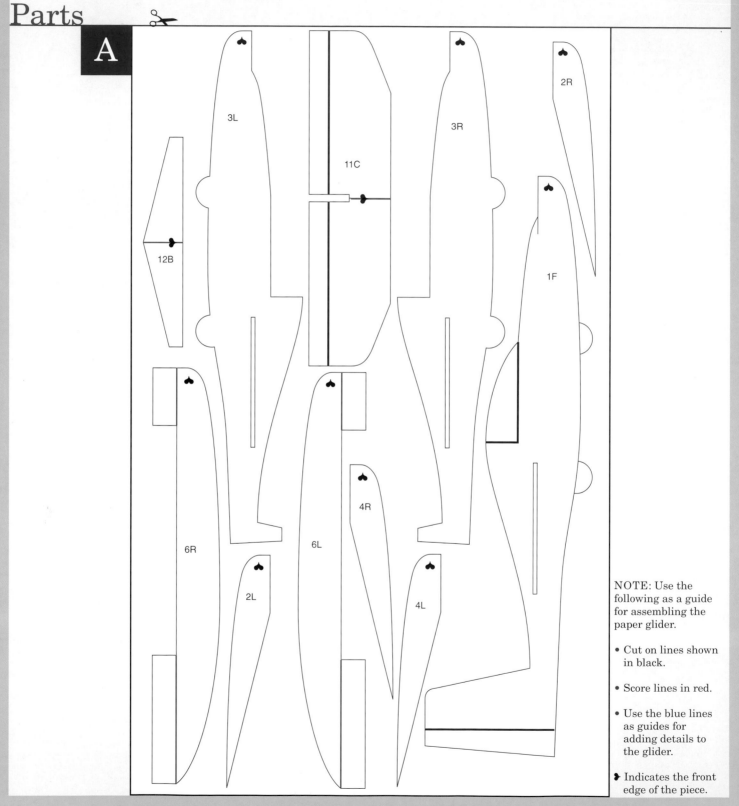

3L

2R

11C

3R

12B

1F

6R

4R

6L

2L

4L

NOTE: Use the following as a guide for assembling the paper glider.

• Cut on lines shown in black.

• Score lines in red.

• Use the blue lines as guides for adding details to the glider.

❥ Indicates the front edge of the piece.

First, photocopy these two pages (100% size).

Then cut out the portion indicated below from the photocopy.
This makes a cutting guide for the various parts and fits a
standard 5 x 8 inch index card. See page 77 for step two.

# Parts

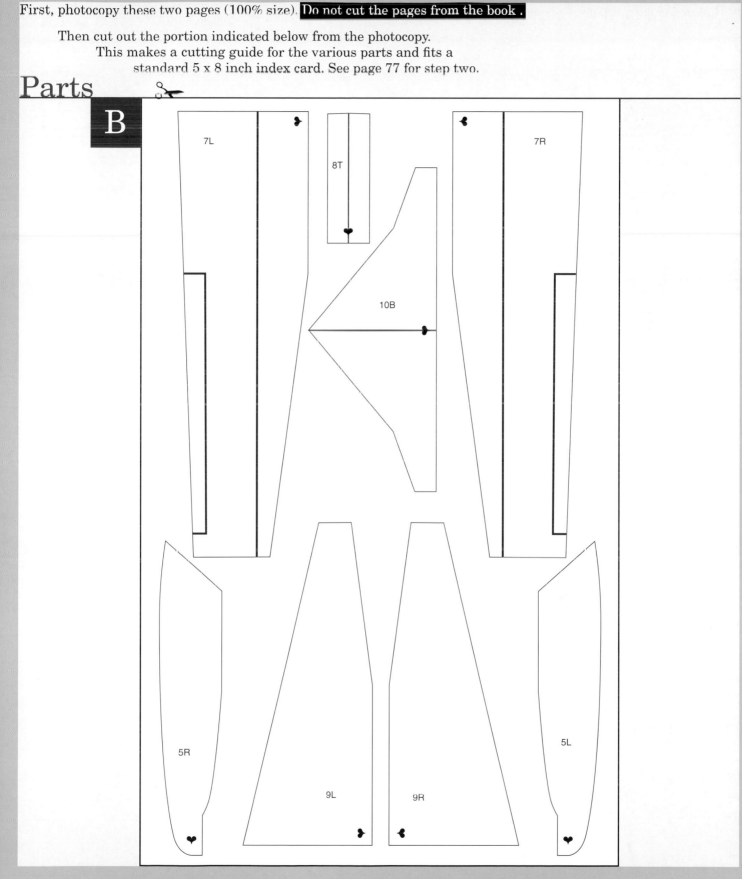

# Genesis

## 14

Jim Marske has been building flying wing aircraft since the 1950s, experimenting with different designs. For the development of this glider he lent his expertise to a team of designers. The result was a hybrid with some features of a regular aircraft, such as vertical and horizontal stabilizers, but with virtually no fuselage like a flying wing. The team used the computer to develop its aerodynamics. Computer assisted design makes very efficient low drag airframes possible. This glider is of fiberglass and kevlar construction. **(See text p 59.)**

# Instructions

NOTE: Also refer to general instructions on pp 6-9.

**1** See pages 82 and 83 for this step.

**2** Tack-glue parts cutting guides onto index cards by gluing on the **back-side between the parts**.

**3** Cut opening for wings in fuselage parts.

**4** Score the fold lines for wing and tail tabs. (After cutting out the pieces, bend tabs outward.)

**5** Cut each piece from the index card stock. Remove light-weight guide paper and discard, leaving a clean unmarked glider part.

NOTE: Cut carefully through both sheets. The cutting side is always the upward or outward facing surface of the finished part.

**6** Glue pieces 1F through 5R and 5L to build up fuselage layers, carefully aligning parts.

NOTE: Ensure that the entire contacting surface of a smaller piece being fastened to a larger one is completely covered with glue.

Press fuselage flat between clean sheets of paper underneath a heavy weight (a few big books) until glue is sufficiently set (about 45 minutes).

**7** Bring wing parts 6R and 6L together, fastening with 7T. Then glue 8R and 8L to the bottom of the wing. Finally glue 9B to the very bottom.

**8** Applying glue to the tail tabs, fasten horizontal stabilizer 10S to the fuselage.

**9** Applying glue to the wing tabs, fasten wing assembly to the fuselage.

**10** Camber the wings by curving the paper gently between thumb and forefinger. See below.

NOTE: Make sure wing parts are aligned along the centerline.

The dihedral angle of the wings must be set before the glue dries. See below.

Dihedral: 2 in (5 cm)

Camber:

point of maximum camber, 30% from front

correct

too much

NOTE: After completing the glider, it is important to let the glue set completely (an hour or two) before flying.

5L, 4L, 3L, 2L, 1F, 2R, 3R, 4R, 5R

6L, 7T, 8L, 6R, 8R, 9B, 10S

## Parts ✂

**A**

3L

9B

2R

2L

3R

1F

7T

10S

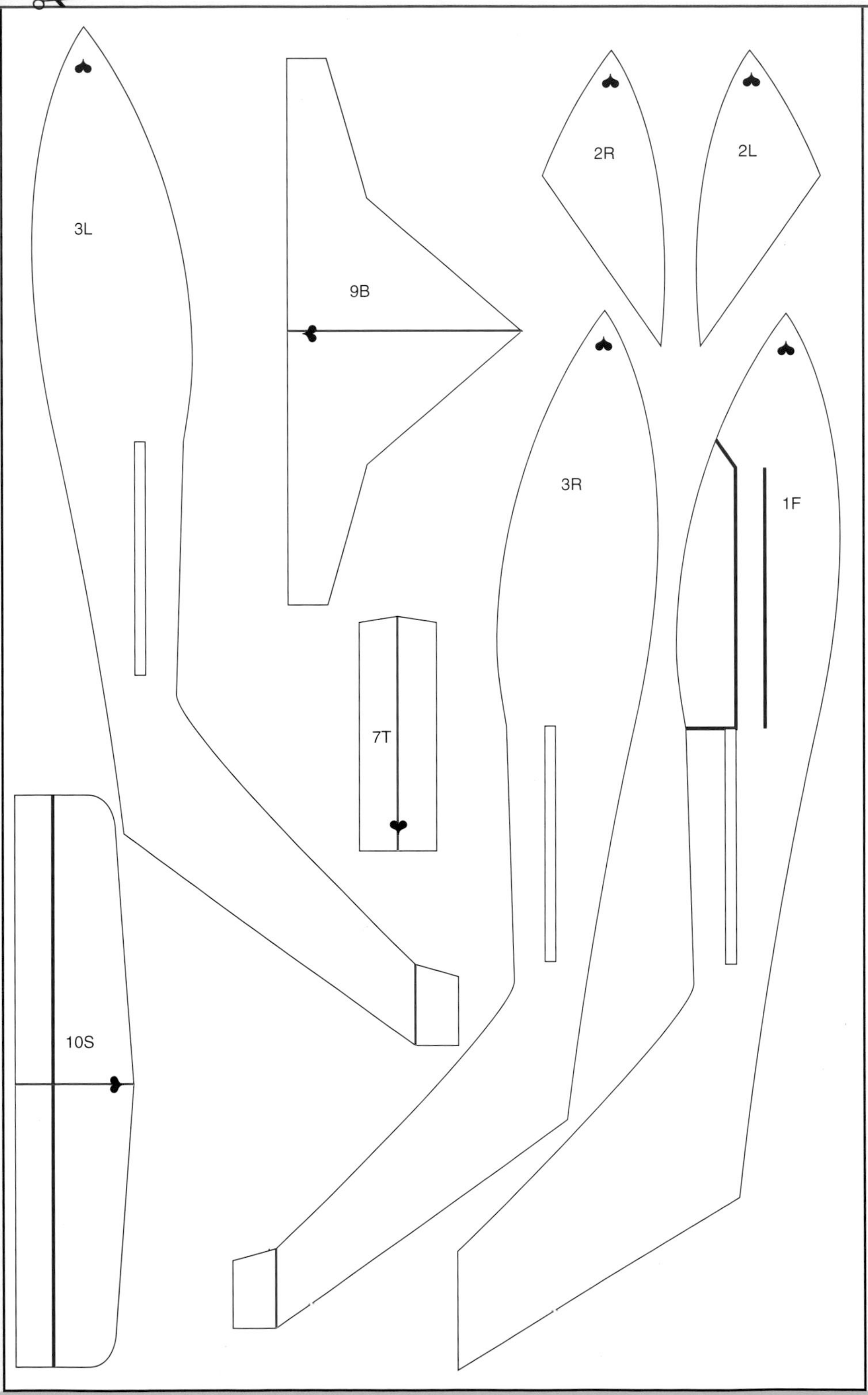

NOTE: Use the following as a guide for assembling the paper glider.

- Cut on lines shown in black.

- Score lines in red.

- Use the blue lines as guides for adding details to the glider.

❥ Indicates the front edge of the piece.

First, photocopy these two pages (100% size). **Do not cut the pages from the book .**

Then cut out the portion indicated below from the photocopy.
This makes a cutting guide for the various parts and fits a
standard 5 x 8 inch index card. See page 81 for step two.

# Parts

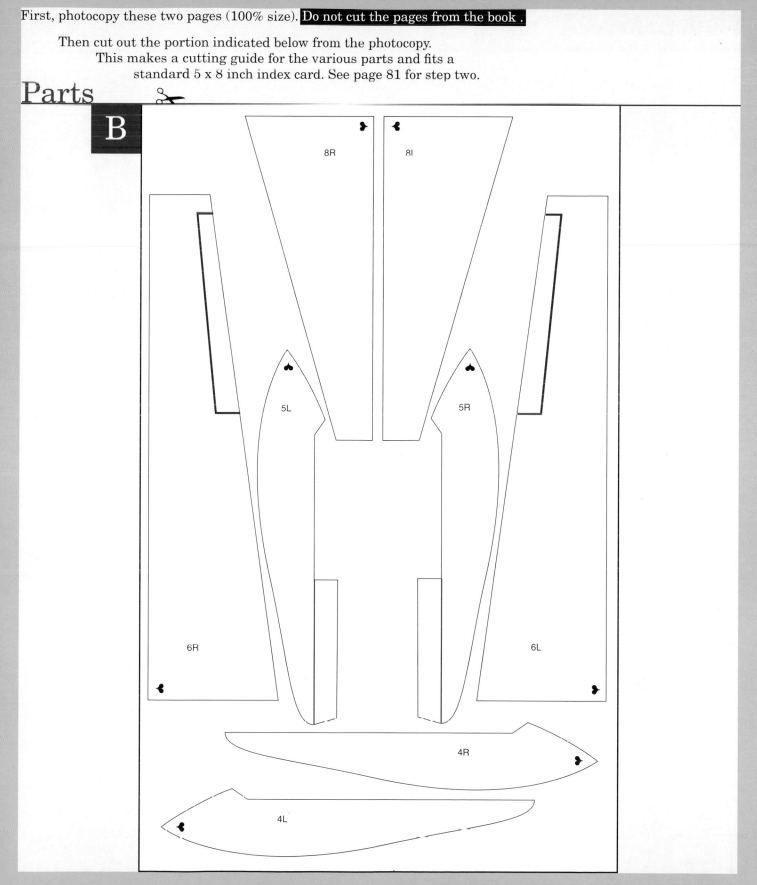

# PW-5 Smyk

## 15

This glider, designed by the Warsaw Technical University in 1993 and certified the following year, introduces a new World Class sailplane. It is designed to be flown by all competing pilots in the Olympic Games of the year 2000, making one-class competition, begun in the U.S. by the Schweizer 1-26, into a world-wide concept. It is designed to be economical — half the cost of a Standard Class glider. It is of all-fiberglass construction, with flight characteristics suited for pilots of all skill levels. **(See text p 59.)**

NOTE: Also refer to general instructions on pp 6-9.

**1** See pages 86 and 87 for this step.

**2** Tack-glue parts cutting guides onto index cards by gluing on the **back-side between the parts**.

**3** Cut opening for wings in fuselage part.

**5** Cut each piece from the index card stock. Remove light-weight guide paper and discard, leaving a clean unmarked glider part.

**4** Score the fold lines for wing and tail tabs. (After cutting out the pieces, bend tabs outward.)

NOTE: Cut carefully through both sheets. The cutting side is always the upward or outward facing surface of the finished part.

6L
5L
4L
3L
2L
1F
2R
3R
4R
5R
6R

**6** Glue pieces 1F through 6R and 6L to build up fuselage layers, carefully aligning parts.

NOTE: Ensure that the entire contacting surface of a smaller piece being fastened to a larger one is completely covered with glue.

Press fuselage flat between clean sheets of paper underneath a heavy weight (a few big books) until glue is sufficiently set (about 45 minutes).

**7** Bring wing parts 7R and 7L together, fastening with 8T. Then glue 9R and 9L to the bottom of the wing. Finally glue 10B to the very bottom.

7L
8T
9L
7R
9R
10D

**8** Applying glue to the tail tabs, fasten horizontal stabilizer 11S to the fuselage.

11S

**10** Camber the wings by curving the paper gently between thumb and forefinger. See below.

NOTE: Make sure wing parts are aligned along the centerline.

The dihedral angle of the wings must be set before the glue dries. See below.

**9** Applying glue to the wing tabs, fasten wing assembly to the fuselage.

point of maximum camber, 30% from front

Camber:

correct

too much

Dihedral: 1 $\frac{1}{2}$ in (3.75 cm)

NOTE: After completing the glider, it is important to let the glue set completely (an hour or two) before flying.

# PW-5 Smyk

## Parts

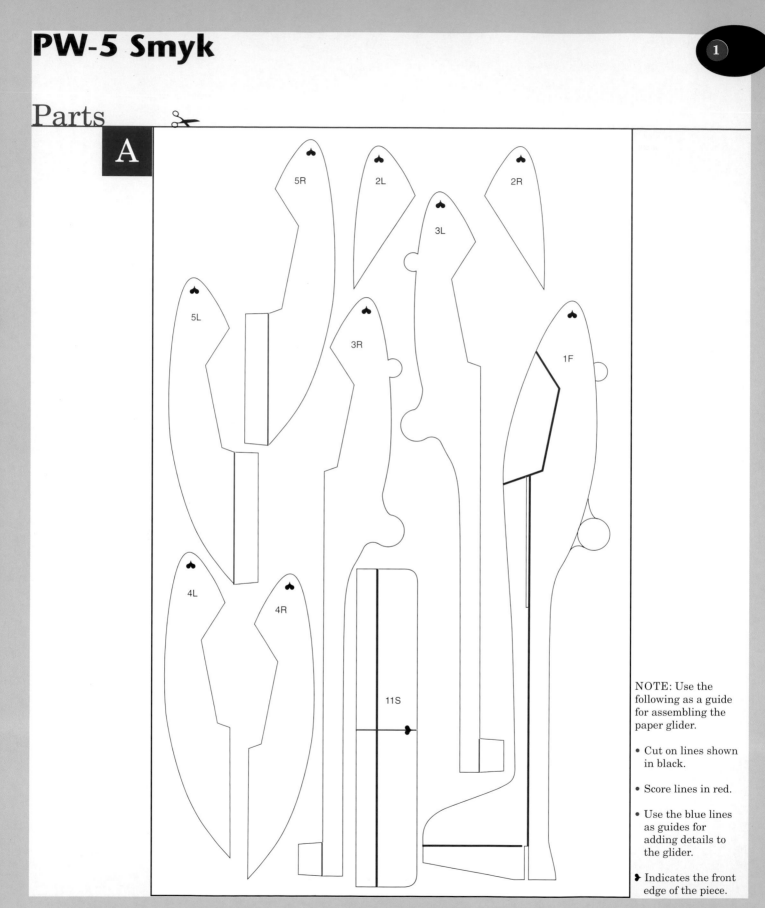

NOTE: Use the following as a guide for assembling the paper glider.

- Cut on lines shown in black.

- Score lines in red.

- Use the blue lines as guides for adding details to the glider.

➤ Indicates the front edge of the piece.

First, photocopy these two pages (100% size). **Do not cut the pages from the book .**

Then cut out the portion indicated below from the photocopy.
This makes a cutting guide for the various parts and fits a
standard 5 x 8 inch index card. See page 85 for step two.

# Parts

## B

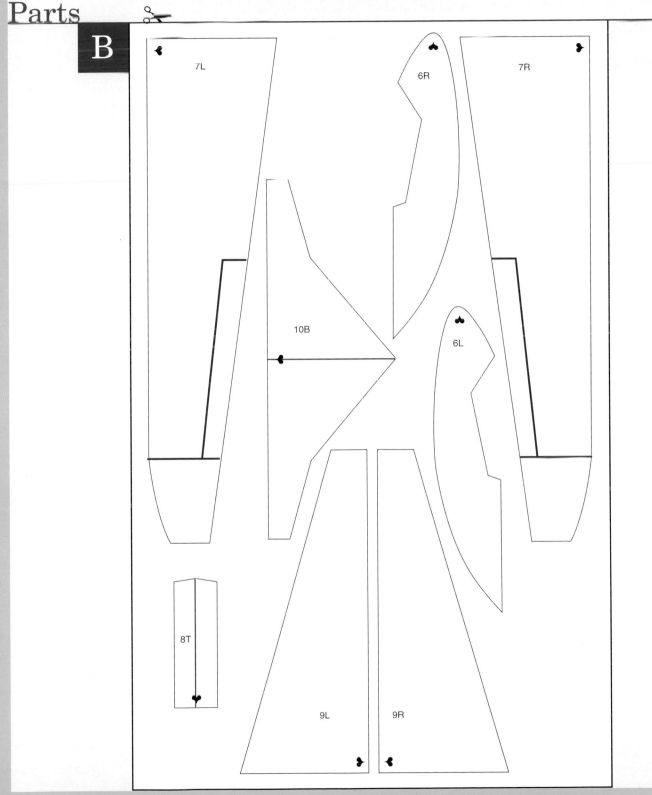

# Schemp-Hirth Nimbus 4

This "supership" is a champion Open Class sailplane, sought after by world-class pilots. Shortly after its introduction, it ranked highest in the first 6 places and second in 9 out of the next 12 in the 1983 World Soaring Championships. This superb aircraft is of carbon fiber construction. It is also available with a motor that pops out of the fuselage behind the cockpit allowing it to remain airborne when no sources of lift are present. **(See text p 59.)**

# Instructions

NOTE: Also refer to general instructions on pp 6-9.

**1** See pages 90 through 92 for this step.

**2** Tack glue parts cutting guides onto index cards by gluing on the **back-side between the parts**.

**3** Cut opening for wings in fuselage parts.

**5** Cut each piece from the index card stock. Remove lightweight guide paper and discard, leaving a clean unmarked glider part.

NOTE: Cut carefully through both sheets. The cutting side is always the upward or outward facing surface of the finished part.

**4** Score the fold lines for wing and tail tabs. (After cutting out the pieces, bend tabs outward.)

**7** Bring wing parts 7R and 7L together, fastening with 8T. Then add 9R + 9L and 10R + 10L to the bottom of the wing. Finally glue 11B and 12B to the very bottom.

NOTE: Ensure that the entire contacting surface of a smaller piece being fastened to a larger one is completely covered with glue.

**6** Glue pieces 1F through 6R and 6L to build up fuselage layers, carefully aligning parts.

Press fuselage flat between clean sheets of paper underneath a heavy weight (a few big books) until glue is sufficiently set (about 45 minutes).

**8** Applying glue to the tail tabs, fasten horizontal stabilizer 13S to the fuselage.

**10** Camber the wings by curving the paper gently between thumb and forefinger. See below.

NOTE: Make sure wing parts are aligned along the centerline.

The dihedral angle of the wings must be set before the glue dries. See below.

**9** Applying glue to the wing tabs, fasten wing assembly to the fuselage.

point of maximum camber, 30% from front

Camber:

correct

too much

NOTE: After completing the glider, it is important to let the glue set completely (an hour or two) before flying.

Dihedral: 2 3/4 in (7 cm)

6L
5L
4L
3L
2L
1F
2R
3R
4R
5R
6R

7L
8T
9L
10L
11L
9R
10R
11R
12B
13S
7R

# Schemp-Hirth Nimbus 4

Parts ✂

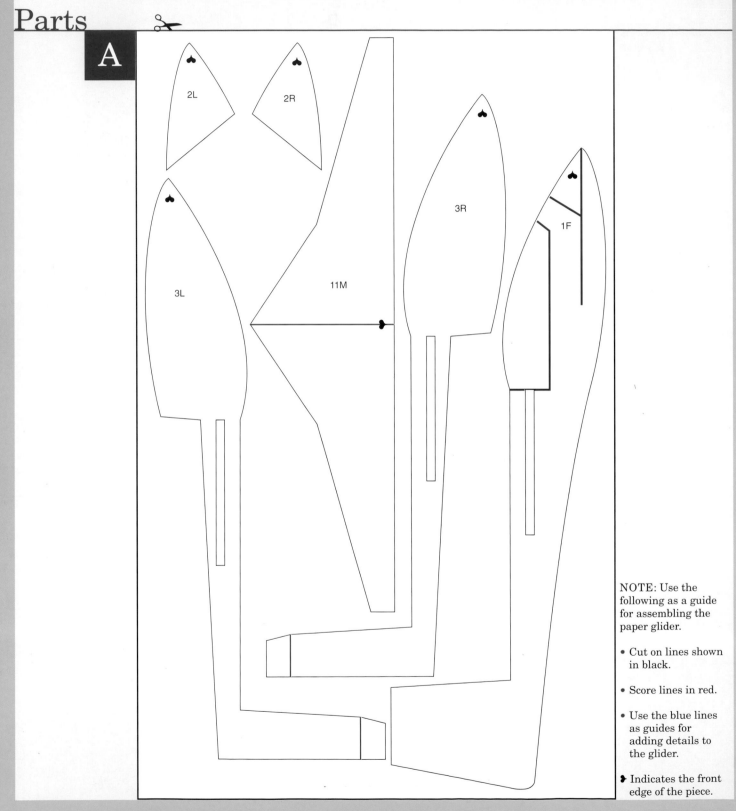

**A**

2L

2R

3R

1F

3L

11M

NOTE: Use the following as a guide for assembling the paper glider.

• Cut on lines shown in black.

• Score lines in red.

• Use the blue lines as guides for adding details to the glider.

❯ Indicates the front edge of the piece.

First, photocopy these two pages and the following page (100% size). Do not cut the pages from the book .

Then cut out the portion indicated below from the photocopy.
This makes a cutting guide for the various parts and fits a
standard 5 x 8 inch index card. See page 89 for step two.

# Parts

**B**

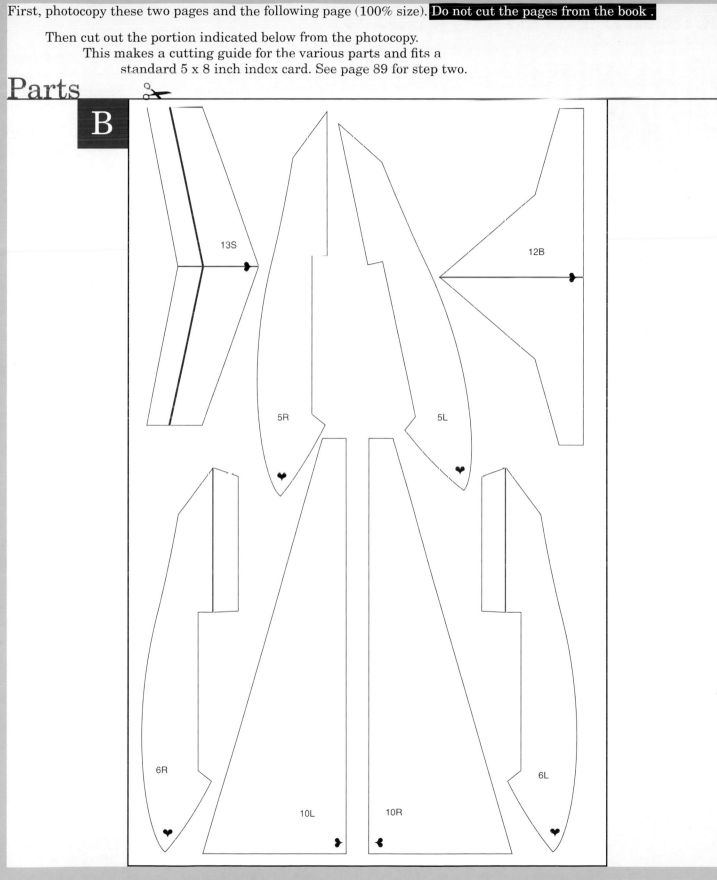

# Schemp-Hirth Nimbus 4

## Parts

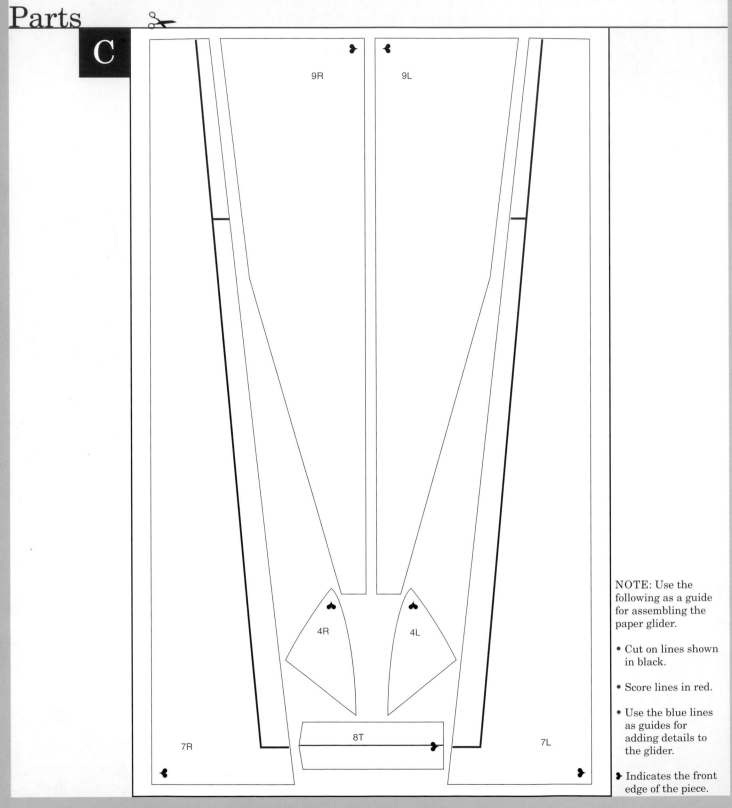

**C**

9R

9L

4R

4L

8T

7R

7L

NOTE: Use the following as a guide for assembling the paper glider.

- Cut on lines shown in black.

- Score lines in red.

- Use the blue lines as guides for adding details to the glider.

➤ Indicates the front edge of the piece.

## HANDLING PAPER GLIDERS

Pick up and hold paper gliders by the nose, their sturdiest part. *Never* lift them by the wings or tail; this will distort their aerodynamic shape.

## PREFLIGHT INSPECTION

After a paper glider is finished and the glue completely dried, do a preflight inspection and make any necessary adjustments.

Examine the glider thoroughly from the front, back, top, bottom, and each side. Check for parts that appear bent or twisted. Correct any defects. Gently massage the paper to work out bends and twists. Each side must be *exactly* like the other — shape, size, camber, dihedral — a paper glider must be symmetrical.

## TEST FLIGHTS

The objective of test flights is to trim (adjust) the glider for straight and level flight at *its best speed*.

Hold the fuselage between thumb and forefinger just behind the plane's center of gravity. Throw it *gently* with a straight ahead motion (not as though it were a baseball). A glider flies best at only one speed. Throwing it too hard will cause it to climb sharply, stall, and dive to the ground, or do a complete loop. Once you have trimmed the glider for good flight performance, different throwing techniques can be tried. Try to test fly in calm conditions so that each flight is more predictable.

Sometimes, on the very first flight, a paper plane is unbalanced in every way at the same time. Therefore it is necessary to separate the control functions in one's mind and deal with them one at a time. (See page 22.)

To correct a dive, in a regular glider, the elevator needs adjusting by bending it up slightly to give positive trim (most of the paper gliders in this book) and down slightly for positive trim in a canard (the Solitaire). Continue making test flights concentrating on this one adjustment until this control input is correct. In normal gliding flight there should be slight positive elevator trim.

If a paper glider banks and turns in either direction it is always due to one wing producing more lift than the other. First make sure that the camber is *identical* in both wings along their entire lengths. If camber is slightly greater in one wing, that wing will produce more lift, causing it to rise — the plane will bank and turn in the opposite direction. Second, make sure that the wings are not twisted. The wingtip that is lower at the trailing edge (thereby having a greater angle of attack) will cause that wing to produce more lift, and it will rise — the plane will bank and turn in opposite direction. Untwist the wings to correct this problem. Continue making test flights concentrating on this adjustment until the wings are correct.

A slightly bent fuselage will also cause the plane to turn by yawing left or right. Make the fuselage as straight as possible. For a final correction adjust the rudder by bending it in the opposite direction to the turn.

The paper gliders in this book are designed to last a long time. To keep them from becoming damaged when not in use they need proper storage. One way is to hang them by the nose from a line using clothes pins.

## POWER LAUNCHING

Just as full-sized gliders were catapulted into the air using shock cords as a source of power in the days before aerotowing, paper gliders can be launched using a catapult made with an elastic band. This is an alternative to the hand-thrown high launch. Using this method, the direction of the launch 45 degrees upward and across the wind is similar to the hand launch method.

First prepare the glider by adding a tow hook. The glue used to build the glider must be *completely* dry for this (at least one day). Use an ordinary map pin (short head pin). Insert it into the nose of the glider in the approximate location shown in figure 15. Additional glue may be needed to keep it in place. To make the catapult, tie an elastic band to a stick such as a wooden dowel. See figure 16.

To launch, hold the glider between thumb and forefinger by the fuselage from underneath at the tail end. Hold the catapult stick in the other hand, loop the elastic over the head of the pin, stretch the band, and release the glider. Care must be taken not to over-speed the glider. If it flutters, use less tension.

## Figure 15

Adding a tow hook

Insert a map pin into the heavy part of a glider's nose, in the direction indicated and as far forward as is practical for each glider type, leaving just the head sticking out. This is the tow hook.

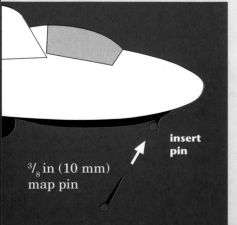

³/₈ in (10 mm) map pin

insert pin

If the glider climbs, loses speed, and pitches down sharply (stalls), the elevator needs to be bent down slightly. However, if this problem cannot be corrected without the elevator being bent down below the straight level, the airplane's center of gravity is too far back and additional ballast is needed in the nose. Glue additional layers of paper into the nose. Again, continue making test flights until this problem is corrected.

Continue to make test flights until the plane flies straight and level in a gentle glide.

## EXTENDING THE GLIDE

Full-sized gliders are always launched into the wind. If a paper glider is launched into the wind the increased relative airspeed would make the lightweight paper glider climb very steeply, and perhaps stall, and dive to the ground, or, if the elevator is bent up slightly, do a complete loop. When launched with the wind, wind speed is added to actual airspeed, increasing the ability to cover distance over the ground. But in a downwind launch the glider may stall if the wind is too strong because of the decreased relative airspeed. To avoid these tendencies, launch the glider across the wind, letting it turn downwind gradually.

Another way to fly a paper glider is to begin the flight with a high launch. The glider should be trimmed for a gentle left or right turn. (If the pilot is right-handed, trim for a gentle turn to the left.) For making a left turn adjust the control surfaces. (See page 22.)

Make these trim adjustments in very slight increments until the desired turn rate is achieved.

Launch the glider in an inclined position with considerable force upward and away from your body (about 45 degrees), across the wind. It gains altitude from the force of the throw, but loses speed as it climbs. The dihedral causes the wings to level out. Once level, the left-handed trim banks the glider into a gentle turn downwind at the top of its climb. Because of the altitude gained by the high launch, the descent should be a good long glide.

With a high launch it is also possible for a paper glider to become a sailplane and soar.

When the sun is shining, thermals can form almost anywhere, especially over dark colored fields, usually between 10 am and 4 pm (see page 36). If, after reaching the top of a launch, the glider spirals inside a bubble of rising air, it will climb even higher and extend its glide if the bubble is rising faster than the glider is descending. Some thermals are stronger than others and rise faster. The paper glider with the best glide ratio will be able to take advantage of the weakest thermals.

Because paper is a relatively unstable material it may be necessary to readjust the planes after every few flights. Gusty wind conditions can occur around strong thermals making it impossible to fly successfully such lightweight planes.

**Aerotow**   Towing a glider behind a powered airplane used as a method of launching the glider.

**Aspect ratio**   The length of a wing in relation to its width. A square has an aspect ratio of 1:1.

**Ailerons**   Surfaces on the trailing edges of the wings that control roll.

**Airfoil**   A wing having a curved upper surface and usually a flat lower surface.

**Angle of attack**   The downward slant, from front to back, of an airfoil to increase lift.

**Angle of bank**   The raising of the outside wing and the lowering of the inside wing during a turn.

**Attitude**   The roll, pitch, and yaw of an aircraft in flight, and the direction it is pointing in relation to the horizon.

**Ballast**   Extra weight in the nose of an aircraft used to adjust the center of gravity.

**Bernoulli's Principle**   The decrease of a fluid's pressure as its rate of flow increases.

**Canard**   An aircraft having a small set of wings ahead of the main wings.

**Camber**   The curved upper surface of a wing.

**Center of gravity**   The point on the aircraft where its weight appears to be concentrated.

**Center of lift**   The point on the aircraft where its lift appears to be concentrated.

**Chord**   The distance from front to back of a wing.

**Control surfaces**   Small flat hinged surfaces on the wings and tail used to maintain equilibrium and maneuver an aircraft.

**Dihedral angle**   The upward slanting of wings away from the fuselage.

**Drag**   The resistance of air on moving objects.

**Elevator**   Control surface on the trailing edge of the horizontal stabilizer used to adjust pitch.

**Fuselage**   The body of an airplane.

**Gravity**   The force of the earth keeping objects on the ground and giving them weight.

**Horizontal stabilizer**   A flat horizontal surface that directs the flow of air in aid of maintaining equilibrium.

**Leading edge**   The front edge of a wing.

**Lift**   The force generated by the wings that counteracts the force of gravity. Also, rising air currents used for soaring.

**Maneuver**   Skilfully making an airplane move in the correct manner and fly in the desired direction.

**Pitch**   The rotation of an airplane causing its nose to go up or down.

**Ridge lift**   Rising air currents over sloping ground used by gliders to remain airborne.

**Roll**   The rotation of an airplane causing the wingtips to rise or fall.

**Rudder**   Control surface on the trailing edge of the vertical stabilizer used to control yaw.

**Shock cord**   An elastic rope used to launch gliders.

**Spar**   The main frame that supports a wing.

**Stall**   The condition that occurs when the angle of attack is too great.

**Streamlining**   Making an airplane's shape smooth so that air can flow across it creating the least amount of drag possible.

**Thermal lift**   Rising air currents over heated ground used by gliders to remain airborne.

**Thrust**   The force needed to move an airplane forward.

**Trailing edge**   The back edge of a wing.

**Trim**   The adjustment of control surfaces so that an airplane in flight does not roll, pitch, or yaw.

**Trim drag**   The drag created by the control surfaces.

**Vertical stabilizer**   A flat vertical surface that directs the flow of air in aid of maintaining equilibrium.

**Vortex**   Air that slips off the wingtips from the high pressure area below to the low pressure area above the wings, and swirls in a circular manner behind each wingtip.

**Wave lift**   Rising air currents over mountains used by gliders to remain airborne.

**Wing loading**   The amount of weight a given area of wing is required to lift.

**Wing span**   The distance from wingtip to wingtip.

**Yaw**   The rotation of an airplane causing its nose to go left or right.

## Figure 16

Elastic band catapult launcher

Tie a long thin elastic band to one end of a short stick such as a wooden dowel. To keep the knot from coming undone, tape it in place.

tape over knot

elastic band

$^1/_{16}$ x $^1/_{16}$ x 6 – 8 in
(1.5 x 1.5 x 150-200 mm)

# Index

## Further Reading

### BOOKS

Mackie, Dan. *Flight: Discover Planes, Hang Gliders, and Ultralights.* Hayes, Burlington, 1986.

Schweizer, Paul A. *Wings Like Eagles.* Smithsonian, Washington, 1988.

Schmidt, Norman. *Discover Aerodynamics With Paper Airplanes.* Peguis, Winnipeg, 1991.

Schmidt, Norman. *Best Ever Paper Airplanes.* Sterling/Tamos, New York, 1994.

Schmidt, Norman. *Super Paper Airplanes.* Sterling/Tamos, New York, 1996.

Taylor, Michael. *History of Flight.* Crescent, New York, 1990.

### PERIODICALS

*Free Flight.* The Soaring Association of Canada. Ottawa, bi-monthly.

*Model Aviation.* Academy of Model Aeronautics. Reston, monthly.

*Sailplane & Gliding.* British Gliding Association. Leicester, bi-monthly.

*Soaring.* The Soaring Society of America. Hobbs, monthly.